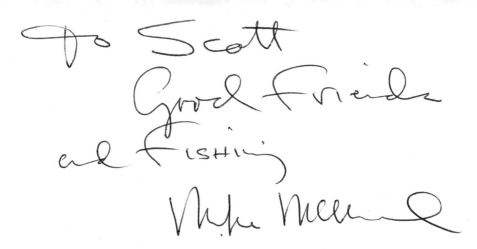

To Scott
Good Friends
and Fishing
Mike McClelland

HOW TO WIN THE WALLEYE GAME

The latest information-packed book on walleye fishing available. Chock-full of practical how-to, when-to, where-to advice. Based on solid research and successful tournament experience from all walleye waters across the U.S. and Canada. For beginners and experts alike.

BY JEFF MURRAY & MIKE MCCLELLAND

Cover Photo and Inside Photography by Jeff Murray, unless noted otherwise
Layout and Design by Jeff Murray and Terry Berendes
Artwork and Illustrations by Gary Eckenberg and Leslie McClelland

D1592520

How to Win the Walleye Game

Copyright © 1988 by Jeff Murray
First Printing December 1988
Second Printing May 1989
Third Printing March 1990
Fourth Printing December 1991
Fifth Printing May 1993
Sixth Printing January 1996
ISBN: 0-9622571-0-9 (Hardcover);
0-9622571-1-7 (Library binding);
0-9622571-3-3 (Softcover)

DEDICATION

To the wives, Darcy McClelland and Corie Murray, where true patience is personified, and whose support is without price. And to the Almighty Creator, and His Son, Who did mankind a mighty big favor when He fashioned and placed walleyes in rivers and lakes.

ACKNOWLEDGEMENTS

The authors wish to thank the following, without which this book would not be a reality: Bob Propst, whose 35 years of chasing walleyes where they'd never been caught before helped accelerate our fishing knowledge; Jerry Anderson, a trusted friend and a straight-shooter, as well as one of the very best fishermen in the nation; Gary Parsons, a superb angler who is the fastest learner we've ever met; Gary Roach and Randy Amenrud, two guys who are *almost* as nice as they are good at catching walleyes; Bob Palser, Bud Riser, Babe Winkelman; the MWC and its "regulars".

Why did I decide to write this book with Jeff Murray? I knew there was a need for another walleye book because I kept catching fish and winning tournaments by doing something "wrong." According to accepted principles, for example, a walleye isn't supposed to be in shallow water during midday when the sun is bright. Happenings like this were considered odd behavior, or accidental catches, but they became rules for me. It wasn't long when I realized that they weren't an oddity; the information was wrong. I felt I could write a book just to do away with the many myths that had become established "laws."

There's only one problem. I'm not a writer. And I wanted the book to be top shelf. The only solution was to find someone who had a way with words and knew walleyes. It wouldn't be easy because whomever I selected had to meet some strict criteria. To begin with, I wanted someone who writes in an easy-to-read, entertaining style, but I wanted it to be blunt; I don't like beating around the bush on the subject of walleye fishing. I also wanted someone who knows how to do hard-core research, and not all writers are good at it. It takes more than an inquisitive mind to penetrate issues.

My search ended when I read several articles by Jeff Murray in *Outdoor Life* magazine. Jeff is an award-winning, nationally-known writer whose favorite fish happens to be the walleye. Many writers have "jumped the bandwagon" lately, because magazines are now recognizing the tremendous growing popularity of this fish. Jeff's passion, however, is genuine and his articles reflect it; he has a long history of providing more solid walleye material for national publications than any other free-lance outdoor writer. I especially like his honest, hard-hitting style. Rather than blab about himself and export his opinions, he uses solid scientific research to back up his beliefs. Clearly, he stands out from the rest, as the best.

But there was a bonus about Jeff: his fishing credentials. He obviously had paid his dues on the water, because what he wrote not only made sense, but paralleled much of my thinking. If that wasn't enough, his photography is outstanding.

Now that I have the book in my hands, I know I made the right decision. I hope you agree!

Sincerely,

Mike

Mike McClelland

FOREWORD —ABOUT THE AUTHORS

The idea of collaborating on a book with Mike McClelland popped into my head within five minutes of my first conversation with the guy. I mean, here was a tournament pro who had the best track record of anyone on the circuit. Mike has twice shared the prestigious MWC Team Of The Year award, he is the current reigning World Champion, two-time Mercury National champion, and winner of dozens of other tournaments held across the country.

Obviously, Mike was doing a lot of things right, but what? I just had to find out. On the surface, however, he appeared to be using essentially the same kinds of equipment and tactics as his competitors. There had to be more, and I couldn't rest until I had unearthed every tidbit of walleye lore from the guy.

I was in for a pleasant surprise when I rolled up the shirt-sleeves and wrote my first few articles incorporating some of Mike's experiences. Mike turned out to be very articulate, with an unusual gift for investigating important issues. Not only did he spend 250 days a year on the water figuring out how to catch walleyes, but he had a refreshing, common sense approach to everything he did. Here was a guy who I could ask, "Why?" and get some straight answers that weren't disguised in vague terms. There was no "mid-meso" monkey business to wade through and no "structural elements" to decipher. What's more, if he didn't know the answer, he'd say so. Occasionally, he'd refer me to one of his tournament competitors. I appreciate humility as much as knowledge.

But the best thing about Mike, from a walleye nut / outdoor writer's standpoint, is that he has some controversial beliefs that collide with much of our modern mainline walleye doctrine. That was exciting! Even though some of his ideas might be unpopular or unconventional, much of my research, based on radio telemetry studies, proved him to be right on the money.

There are a lot of walleye books on the market these days. A few are pretty good, but most are mediocre. And Lord knows, the world doesn't need another mediocre walleye book. I think we've put together one of the best. Here's hoping you agree.

Sincerely,

Jeff Murray

PREFACE—THE WALLEYE *GAME?*

Win the walleye game? What game? Tournaments? We know what you're thinking. You question the idea of mixing competition with fishing. Add money to the affair, and people sometimes do naughty things—like horn in on another guy's spot. Or beat him to it the next day out. It's true, tournament fishing isn't for everyone. There's no question that competition can taint the pure, gentlemanly sport of angling. Not all agree on the subject. I dislike a lot of things associated with fishing tournaments, while Mike literally thrives on them. But there are a few things we can all agree on.

One is that whether you realize it or not, you're competing—your wits matched against those of the fish. Only, if you lose, you don't risk your life. You're also competing against other fishermen in a very real sense. Fishing pressure modifies fish behavior, and you can't always have a particular lake, much less a specific spot, all to yourself. The more you know the rules of the walleye game, however, the more you'll come out on top.

Second, the motivation to win causes man to rise above the average and reach beyond himself. Whether he's seeking personal satisfaction, recognition, or dollars, is really immaterial. If he discovers something of value, all may benefit. Can you imagine someone with raised eyebrows and puckered lips saying, "I'm not going to try that technique, even though it works, because it was discovered during a tournament."?

Now, it's entirely possible to unlock a walleye mystery or two while the wife and kids are along on a leisurely Sunday afternoon outing. But when the heat is on and anglers *have* to produce, innovative tactics and interesting discoveries are more often the result; when all the old, reliable methods fail, "tossing out the book," and going for broke is more than appropriate. Al Lindner once explained why he enjoys a tournament atmosphere. "Put 200 boats on a good fishery all at once," he said, "and it's like being in 200 places at the same time. You can learn more in one day than in a whole summer." He's right!

Like I said, tournament fishing isn't for everyone. *But the knowledge gained is.* Recently, I chatted with Ricky Clunn, one of the best bass tournament anglers of all time. When asked how far man's fishing knowledge has progressed, he said, "On a scale of one to 10, probably three." As far as walleyes are concerned, we believe this book will take us to step four.

Fifty tournament teams... or 50 research teams?

Contents

Contents Continued ...

Part I

THE WALLEYE MYSTIQUE

"Gee, with this bright sun, the walleyes gotta be deep."

Walleye Mania strikes again.

CHAPTER 1
WHY WALLEYES?

Of the 21,000-odd species of fish, none is making as many waves in America as the walleye. The beloved largemouth bass is gradually being replaced by the walleye as the nation's number-one fish. There was a time that the fishing tackle industry only listened to—and targeted—bass anglers. Today, walleye fishermen are gaining inroads to product development like never before. Why all the fuss? Simple. The walleye is *the* fish of the future. If there are no quality walleye fisheries near you at the present time, chances are good that there could be one in a few short years.

How's that? The walleye, unlike the bass or trout, is very adaptable. Although it is originally a fish of the Midwest and Canada, it has proven itself in waters out West, in the East and down South. The walleye is equally at home in a natural lake, a river or a reservoir. And positive changes on all three scenes are helping to spread the walleye gospel, which declares that this fish is fun to catch for the whole family, and one of the finest on the dinner table.

Consider reservoirs. Every time the Army Corps of Engineers builds another impoundment, a new, hot walleye fishery—one that's here to stay—develops. The reason is simple walleye biology. Walleyes don't need overhead cover for survival, as do crappies and bass. Instead, all they need is a decent forage base and some "spawning rocks." They often get all they need in most impoundments; flooded roadways, bridge embankments and rip rap along the face of the dam will do nicely. Meanwhile, flooded timber and brush, preferred by largemouth and panfish, are doomed in time as they decompose and become silted over. And those fish populations linked to them are destined to decline along with them.

Some of the hottest walleye fishing in the nation right now is in our Western reservoirs, in the states of New Mexico, Texas, Wyoming, Colorado and Montana. And overstuffed fish in the 20-pound range continue to be caught in our older reservoirs in the South. Even if spawning rocks are lacking, the fish are easily stocked in impoundments.

Which is why the story on natural lakes is also encouraging—walleyes are an excellent hatchery fish. You can strip them right on their spawning site and hatch them economically and efficiently with portable incubators utilizing water from a garden hose. In a few weeks time, millions of fry can be released in prospective waters. And if the local game manager's research indicates low survival rates are the rule on Lake Nolimit, raising fry to the fingerling stage in nearby rearing ponds can increase the ratios. Intensive research, conducted in recent years, will result in better stocking programs. They will be needed. Fishing pressure will continue to rise.

Rivers have always been an untapped resource for many gamefish, but programs implementing the Clean Water Act, initiated in the early '70s, are creating new walleye fisheries overnight. The Fox River in Wisconsin, the Tittabawassee River (and Saginaw Bay) in Michigan, and the Illinois River south of Chicago are but a few examples. Cleaner water = more walleyes.

Walleye distribution is expanding across the country, as a result of these factors. But there's another one that could make the walleye the hottest fish, even in the South. Some good ol' boys might be switching over to Marble Eyes sooner than they think. The reason is the zander, the walleye's European look-alike cousin. Zanders can handle softer water and higher temperatures, and they might be able to naturally reproduce in Southern reservoirs, where the walleye now can't. To boot, the zander grows considerably larger than the walleye; the European record is reportedly 44 pounds, and 12 to 20 pounders here should be common. North Dakota is now experimenting with them on a limited basis (three other states are considering future zander projects). This is a heckuva fish with a bright future.

Even if walleyes weren't gaining in popularity and distribution, you should learn to catch them if you like kids. Walleye fishing is more of a participant sport than a spectator or competitive one. It's fairly laid back because marathon casts and 150-horse engines are not necessary requirements of the game. Conversation usually flows naturally in a walleye boat and at the boat landing. It's a quality experience with ample opportunity to communicate with one another. And building positive memories is a natural by-product of an outing after walleyes—everybody usually gets into the act. Walleyes aren't tough to catch, once you find them, and Dad won't always outfish Mom and the kids.

Walleyes are good for the economy, too. Just when the boat market got saturated, along came another fishery with another set of likes and dislikes. Flat-bottomed models are no longer the rage; the deep-V, walk-through windshield is a hot item. Thus, new designs led to new jobs. The same goes for lures. Three bass crankbait-oriented lure companies—Bill Norman, Rebel and Bomber—have especially prospered from the walleye craze.

But many people outside the fishing industry, particularly those in the oil states, have been saved by the walleye. When it was economically feasible to drill more oil wells a few years ago, states such as Texas, New Mexico, Colorado, Montana and the Dakotas experienced an economic boom. But with falling oil prices, many jobs have been lost. Because walleye fishermen are highly mobile, and their communication network is tremendous, many communities located near walleye fisheries in these states have been revitalized. When the word gets out that five-pound fish are biting on Conches Reservoir in New Mexico, for example, a week later hundreds of boats will show up. Restaurants, motels and baitshops fill to overflowing. A couple of weeks later, in Saginaw Bay, Michigan, the same phenomenon will occur if the walleyes go on a hot streak.

Finally, walleyes will be number-one for a long, long time because they're so good to eat. Fillet of sole is a favorite seafood dish, but do you know what many restaurant menus call it? That's right, the "saltwater walleye." (By the way, when's the last time you saw bass listed on the menu?) Here's a challenge: Eat *one* walleye fillet on an empty stomach, and try to leave a second one alone. On a recent fact-finding trip to a Texas Reservoir, we invited Wade Bourne, a talented Tennessee-based outdoor writer along. Guess how many walleye fillets he ate at a single setting? Try 14. And they were solid, two-pound fish. Need we say more?

So why kid yourself? The walleye is the fish of the future, and there's no reason to miss out on a growing trend that makes a lot of sense.

When it comes to eating walleyes, Wade Bourne has no self-control. But can you blame him?

THE DIRTY DOZEN

Simply put, the growing popularity of walleye fishing nationwide has created an unfathomed thirst for more walleye knowledge. Until recently, most of this knowledge has been unavailable or misinterpreted. If you disagree, consider the following questions. Quickly, just answer "yes" or "no."

1. Do walleyes nibble or suck on a bait?
2. Do walleyes prefer deep water?
3. Do they prefer rocky bottoms over weeds or wood (logs, brush)?
4. Are walleyes benthic (bottom-dwelling) fish?
5. Are walleyes lazy swimmers (territorial)?
6. Does light hurt their eyes?
7. Do walleyes bite better at night?
8. Can they see better in muddy or murky water?
9. Are walleyes color-selective?
10. Are they line shy?
11. Are small hooks better for hooking walleyes with live bait?

12. Are commercial scents effective?

If you answered "yes" to any of the above questions, you've got some re-thinking to do, and this book will help. These are the "dirty dozen" misconceptions that have painted a mysterious, somewhat mystical picture on the canvass of most walleye fishermen's minds. We call it the walleye mystique, and it's a very distorted picture, indeed. Walleyes are as straightforward as you're going to find in the world of fishing. Once located, few gamefish are as easy to catch.

Exposing the first myth is most crucial, because it lays the foundation for our system of fishing. Without a proper understanding of how walleyes feed, it's virtually impossible to rise above mediocrity. And as angling pressure increases, fishing will only get tougher. So there's a constant need to improve.

The next four myths deal with walleye location. Their significance is a close second. If there is an unchanging, unbending rule to the game of walleye fishing, it's that *you can't catch a fish that isn't there* ; virtually every other rule has an exception. Regrettably, these myths have helped create a generation of badly misinformed fishermen; today's fast-food-oriented angler wants cut-and-dried, surefire formulas for filling his livewell. That's a tall order to fill. It would be nice to come up with a list of simple do's and don'ts for finding walleyes, but there are more exceptions than rules!

Next, we must deal with those myths that have been perpetrated about the walleye's much-talked-about vision. They're roadblocks on the highway to walleye heaven; they won't necessarily keep you from catching fish, as some of the others might, but your journey will take longer with all the detours. Indeed, one look at a walleye's reflective, bewitching eyeballs will tell you that he's different from other gamefish. But how different?

And finally, there are a few myths that have gained popularity because a TV celebrity or a big name in the industry endorsed a particular product or method when, in reality, there might be a better way.

Sacred, long-held beliefs, no matter how far they are from the truth, don't die easy. And some of them may appear to be valid for a specific geographic region, but that doesn't give us the right to make a rule out of them. The more we fish walleyes, the more we learn that there's so much to unlearn.

So first, some unlearning.

CHAPTER 2
HOW WALLEYES EAT

Nothing is so misunderstood, yet so important in the world of walleye fishing, as how walleyes eat. It forms the foundation of our entire school of thought, and it affects everything we do on the water.

A walleye is primarily an ambush feeder, relying on cover—structure, low light—to get close to its prey. After improving its position, the fish merely sucks water through its gills...and there goes another meal.

Let's start out with a bang: It's a lie that "walleyes nibble." We've spent enough time observing how walleyes take a bait to know better. Like Yogi Berra says, "You can observe a lot just by watching." Mike's done a lot of that on the clear-water tail-races below the Oahe Dam in South Dakota, and so have I in many North Country lakes in the winter through an ice hole.

If walleyes don't nibble, you ask, then why do we so often get half a night crawler back after a legitimate bite? Are walleyes clumsy, or what? A good question, no doubt, that's sure to open a can of worms. No, walleyes do not nibble, and the reason you get half a crawler (or a tooth-marked leech or minnow) back without a fish, is your fault. Not the fish's.

Walleyes typically eat like most "ambush" feeders: from a strategic place, in a specific manner. Structure—rocks, weeds, stumps—help them to do this by allowing them to hide from their prey. Then, when unsuspecting baitfish swim a wee bit too close, a walleye will slowly improve his position along the structure and inhale the bait. Sounds elementary, but it's quite profound.

What walleyes don't do is lash out and bust up the school of baitfish; salmon are "slashers" that quickly return for cripples. Nor do walleyes dash out and chase their prey with short, powerful bursts; muskies and northern pike are "chasers." No, a walleye merely eases closer and flares his gills open to draw the surrounding water into his mouth and through his gills. Because the minnow is neutrally-buoyant—it neither sinks nor floats—it goes with the flow, and the walleye captures another meal with no more energy expended than necessary.

Indeed, walleyes are capable predators. But if they didn't suck water like this, they couldn't eat. In fact, they'd probably starve, because they'd be on a par with you trying to catch a minnow in a bathtub with your bare hand. Try it and see how time-consuming *and* tiring it can be!

What's all this have to do with catching walleyes? Everything. You must realize that when you attach your line to a bait or lure, you neutralize the walleye's main weapon for capturing its prey; the line interferes with the natural flow of water, preventing the fish from sucking in your offering. So it's your fault when a fish short-hits you. Once you fully comprehend this vital truth, you'll begin to change the way you fish walleyes—from crankbaits to jigs—and you'll catch more fish.

You see, a walleye never decides to eat half a night crawler for lunch. He sucks the water surrounding the bait, and it starts to flow into his mouth when your line tightens up. Suddenly you feel a "tick" and the bait stops. The fish is certainly not smart enough to avoid the hook. On the contrary, he makes an honest attempt to capture the bait but, with some of the presentations many anglers use, short hits are inevitable.

LETTING, NOT MAKING FISH BITE

What are we to do, fish by remote control? The only anti-dote is concentrating on *letting* fish bite—not *making* them bite—every time you go fishing. If you learn how to do this with all of your presentations, your catches will improve dramatically. We can't make fish bite! But we can catch more of those that do. That's essentially how to win the walleye game—play the odds by using the most efficient tactic and hooking every fish that bites.

A good example of letting fish eat, and not letting them eat, involves jigfishing. If you've done much leadhead jigging, you know that all of your hits come as the jig falls. Some folks mistakenly conclude that walleyes "like" falling objects. The truth is, walleyes often hit a jig when it's rising, but there's a big difference between the two offerings. When your jig is falling, it can be easily siphoned into the fish's mouth. However, when you raise your rod tip, you probably pull the jig out of the fish's mouth, without feeling a thing. In fact, most of the time we don't feel the fish take our jigs; the fish will suddenly "be there." Or, we'll sense something "different," and instinctively set the hook. If you should feel a tick, though, by all means set the hook pronto. It doesn't get any better than that.

We not only cannot make a walleye bite, but we cannot *feel* him bite. What we're sensing is him sucking water and stretch-ing our line out until it "ticks." To become a better fisherman, you've got to discard the notion of giving a fish line after he hits, "so he can chew on it awhile and maybe swallow it." Rather, picture ways to give the fish line *before* he hits your bait. The best way to do it with live bait rigs is to present them with slack between the weight and the bait. This is covered in detail in Chapter 12. And jigs? That's even easier, but first a few thoughts on how a fish's metabolism affects its feeding habits.

Fish, being cold-blooded organisms, are like the water they inhabit; they're either hot (aggressive), lukewarm (neutral) or cold (negative). We call these attitudes, or moods. Now the hotter a fish is, the harder he's going to suck water through his gills, and the more water he's going to displace. The reverse is also true—colder fish don't move nearly as much water when they inhale a bait. That's why on a good day everybody catches fish, and on a bad day only the veterans seem to connect. There's no telling how many fish made passes at lures or baits, but were never detected because the pickup was barely discernable! Only those anglers with perfect presentations catch fish on tough days.

THE NOTION OF NEUTRAL BUOYANCY

If you're catching our drift, a perfect presentation is one that reflects the underwater world of a fish. It will go with the flow so the fish can easily inhale it. Bear in mind that we're not talking about making your jig *look* like a real minnow. In recent years, far too much emphasis has been placed on the appearance of lures and baits, and not enough on their physical properties and their performance.

Remember when the new photo finishes first came out a few years back? Did they help slay the local fish population? And what about the color-selection craze launched in the summer of '86—did having a kaleidoscope of colors in all your jigs and crankbaits really make that much difference? These "advancements" didn't add many fish to the stringer because they majored in minor matters and didn't address the basic biological facts of how walleyes eat.

Since everything a fish eats neither sinks nor floats, shouldn't we tailor our offerings accordingly? After all, if a walleye is used to sucking in only so many cubic inches of water to capture his prey, how can we expect him to work twice as hard for our heavy jigs (and overly-buoyant crankbaits)? Again, on a good day he might, which is at best, one day out of 10.

But leadhead jigs sink, you say. How can we make them neutrally-buoyant? We can't, at least not 100 percent. Here's a clue: What about when the jig falls? Aha, by fishing a jig on the drop as much as possible, rather than dragging it, or swimming it, you'll catch more cold fish. It takes a flawless presentation to hook those that lethargically inhale your bait with the enthusiasm of a child eating spinach.

But don't stop there. The lighter the offering, the farther it will move on a light hit. Surely so-called "crappie jigs" (1/16-ounce to 1/32-ouncers) ought to be renamed "walleye jigs." They're harder to fish with (you won't feel a "tunk" on every drop of the rod tip, as with heavier jigs), but they catch more fish.

Light line also helps. We rarely fish with anything heavier than six-pound-test. Four-pound is a staple for jigging. Although we might break off an occasional big fish on the hook set, we catch way more that hit in the first place. The reason is that light line has less resistance, or drag, in the water. The fish can move our jigs a lot farther if they're tied to thin-diameter line. It has nothing to do with line visibility, and "spooking" fish.

Another way to improve a jig's "buoyancy" is to give it more mass. By "bulking up" the dressing, you can make a jig grab more water as it is drawn toward the mouth of a walleye. All you have to do is take the larger grub body off, say, a quarter-ounce Fuzz-E-Grub, and dress it onto the shank of a smaller Fuzz-E-Grub. When a walleye inhales it, the larger body (which adds little weight but more bulk) will grab the surrounding water and go with the flow more easily. It's a simple law of hydrodynamics. Weight is important, but so is shape.

Doctored crankbaits, typically floating models made to rise a little slower, have been around for at least a dozen years. But the reason they can be deadly on cold-water fish hasn't been explained very well. Again, cold-blooded walleyes need more time and all the help you can give them to get the bait all the way in their mouths. Warm-water fish don't need as much assistance. It's important to know the principle behind doctoring a minnow-imitator, not just how to do it, and we'll cover them both in Chapter 14.

The same goes with Lindy rigging. It's probably the most widely used tactic on walleyes. But we know ways to increase its potency, because we know its Achilles' heel. Hint: walleyes don't nibble. Chapter 12 tackles this one.

CHAPTER 3
WHERE THE WALLEYES ARE

The second-most important principle in the world of walleye fishing is finding fish. Shortly, we'll discuss many practical ways to do just that. But first, a few myths have to die.

Shallow water vs. deep water. That walleyes are by nature a shallow-water fish should come as no surprise. They originally spread to lake systems from rivers, and rivers are, for the most part, quite shallow. Still, the myth lingers and causes doubts. We're told that fish in shallow water are temporary residents, and that they really prefer deeper water that "filters harsh light" from their sensitive eyes (another myth exposed fully in the following chapter). Further, we've been told that when walleyes are found in the shallows, it's because they're making an evening migration, after spending most of their daylight hours in deeper water. This standard dogma is accepted by many respected authorities, including biologists and guides.

Most of it is wrong. If we expect to take on the heavyweights over this issue, we better have a lot of ammunition. We've got both barrels loaded.

Barrel No. 1: Radio-tagging studies prove that walleyes spend more time in shallow water than in deep water. Until recent years, much of our walleye theory was just that—theory. Now we have the technical ability to surgically implant a transmitter inside a fish and monitor its comings and goings over a period of weeks, months or years. As long as the fish is alive and the transmitter continues to send out a signal, we can learn where walleyes like to spend their time.

Data from the first few studies, however, did as much harm as good; either few fish were tracked, or the number of "fixes" received were not sufficient to draw accurate generalities.

For example, six walleyes were tagged and tracked in an Iowa lake in 1978, and in another study three were tracked in northern Minnesota in 1981. One researcher concluded that walleyes have a definite home range, while the other believed that they tend to inhabit particular areas of a lake. Numerous other studies could be cited to "prove" other behavioral characteristics. The temptation to jump to conclusions based on alleged scientific data has been too tempting for some writers to

Conventional methods relied on recapture (and death) of the fish (above).

(Below) Ultrasonic transmitters can be surgically implanted and give continuous read-outs of fish locations.

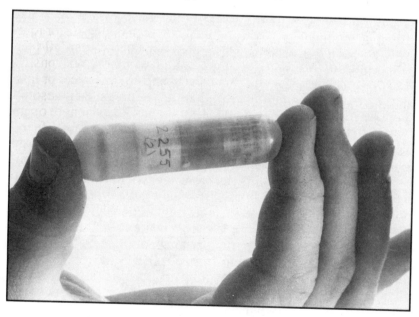

resist. Unfortunately, this often led to the birth of more myths, rather than true education.

Of all the radio-tagging studies, two really stand out for providing fishermen with something reliable to go on. One was conducted on Chautauqua Lake in western New York from April, 1978 to July, 1980. Eighty walleyes were radio-tagged, and over 4,400 locations were obtained on this natural lake. We'll be citing tidbits from this report throughout the book. But for now, let's glean one fact from Don Einhouse's Master of Science thesis, namely, what the average depth of most walleyes tracked was. Would you believe six to 12 feet? The most common depth reported was nine feet, with twice as many fixes for this figure than for any other.

The other research report was done on Meredith Reservoir, near Amarillo, Texas. Here, only 10 walleyes were implanted with ultrasonic transmitters, but all were big fish—from five to 10 pounds. Also, they were tracked weekly (and daily during spring spawning) for over two years. (Note: Chapter 8 contains detailed charts of exactly where these fish went at various times of the year.) Result? More fish were located in water from one to 10 feet than in any other zone (38 percent), with 10 feet to 20 feet being the next-most-frequent zone. In total, 71 percent of the time walleyes were found in less than 20 feet of water, and one individual spent 90 percent of its time in less than 10 feet.

Barrel No. 2 is undisputable, on-the-water results: Men like Mike McClelland and Jerry Anderson keep winning major tournaments without wetting a line in water deeper than 10 feet. Take both of Mike's Mercury National wins on Wisconsin's Lake Winnebago. Most of his fish came from three feet or less. Jerry catches more walleyes than anybody on Minnesota's popular Mille Lacs Lake, where he'll often guide an entire open-water fishing season "without fishing deeper than 10 feet." Jerry's sterling 1988 MWC win on Lake Winnebago was no fluke. He took his fish from 2 1/2 feet of water with slip bobbers, although the majority of contestants were fishing deep because the winning team the previous year trolled crankbaits on leadcore line 17 feet down (Winnebago doesn't get much deeper than 20 feet).

Joe Kraii, Texas fisheries biologist, points to a frequently visited area on one of dozens of Lake Meredith telemetry charts. Hottest areas were typically much shallower than most anglers expect. See Chapter 8 for detailed charts.

Why do we consistently find big walleyes shallow? Because that's where the food is. When it's suppertime, where will you be—in your living room or in your kitchen? There's a distinct advantage to working over a fish that's in shallow water. He's there primarily to eat. And he'll be easier to catch, day in and day out, than one that's in deeper water. This is an important principle worth noting.

It's hard to argue with success. And when scientific facts substantiate anglers' results, myths have to go.

Rocks vs. weeds and wood. Another popular myth with a shaky foundation is that walleyes are a hard-bottom, rock-oriented fish. In some instances, this may appear to be the case but, when given a chance, they'll choose weeds or even wood first. Both studies bear this out. Further, the conclusions of one researcher were the opposite of what we've been led to believe about structure and walleyes. Don Einhouse writes:

"Structure has been used by both anglers and fisheries biologists in describing the preferred habitats of walleye. Typical walleye habitat has been described as firm substrata near bars or points with steep gradients. These types of habitat are available along the east shore of Chautauqua Lake's north basin. However, relatively few walleye radio-locations occurred in these areas. In this study, most walleyes were found in shallower water than expected, based on several life history studies... Although nomadic fish resided over deep water, these large individuals accounted for only a small portion of the lake's total population. Most walleyes in Chautauqua Lake resided in areas near the weedline. Therefore, factors other than substrate or gradient are more important in walleye habitat selection..."

In other words, here's a good walleye lake with a decent dose of rocky drop-offs that are relatively ignored by walleyes. Why? Apparently, the fish are able to feed more efficiently along the weedline. And this natural lake is hardly an isolated case. We could cite many other examples.

What about wood? The Texas study revealed that flooded reservoirs provide excellent cover for walleyes in shoreline brush. Biologist Joe Kraai said that Meredith Reservoir "...has plenty of rocky points and humps... but big walleyes seem to spend more time near flooded brush than rocky drop-off areas." The number of fixes in shoreline brush was about equal to those found on rocky shorelines *and* humps combined!

*Wood Walleyes? Yes they would! Larry Comstock with a huge
stringer of fish taken from downed timber.*

Again, fishing experiences drawn from pressure situations agree with this study. In 1987 and 1988 northern Wisconsin hosted an MWC tournament on the Ciscoe Chain of Lakes, where downed cedar and pine punctuated the shoreline. Most fish registered during both tournaments came from the shade of downed timber.

So don't get hung up on the walleyes/rocks myth. Rocks are good places to fish, but sometimes you can find more fish—and bigger fish—in other places. Weeds and wood top the list.

Suspended vs. bottom. Everyone knows that walleyes are a bottom-hugging species, right? We're not trying to throw a curveball here, but there are exceptions. It's wise to keep them in mind so we don't overlook a segment of a water body's fish population. Yes, in most situations, a presentation close to the bottom will catch more fish than one that's well above it. The exception is when you have a suspended forage base.

A recent Michigan stomach contents study, as part of a very intensive research project on Saginaw Bay, coughed up a few interesting insights. A full 40 percent of the walleyes examined contained identifiable prey fish. Alewife (48 %), smelt (28%), and gizzard shad (26%) predominated. All three species are pelagic (suspending) forage fish in the Bay. Although there are plenty of benthic (bottom-oriented) prey available—spottail shiners, yellow perch, johnny darter and trout perch—walleyes appear to be ignoring them.

This phenomenon seems to confound the fact that most anglers in Saginaw Bay have enjoyed good success with traditional bottom-hugging techniques, including Lindy rigging and jigging. The $64 question is obvious: What will happen when these folks start using Lake Erie-type tactics? Will weight-forward spinners, downriggers and trolling boards greatly increase the catch?

Mike's faithful partner, Bob Propst, proved many years ago that one way to consistently harness reservoir walleyes with a gizzard shad forage base, is to look for suspended fish. Propst would routinely catch fish "in the middle of nowhere" with downriggers and slab spoons while most anglers stuck to shoreline structure and conventional methods. Bud Riser, publisher of *Walleye* magazine, has helped pioneer and expose the suspended walleye fishery elsewhere. Furthermore, he insists that many natural lakes have an untapped resource in suspended walleyes. Don Einhouse did find large fish over deep water in his Chautauqua Lake study, although their numbers weren't great.

Bob Propst, grand master of the walleye world, has pioneered many modern tactics we have come to take for granted.

Territorial, lazy swimmers? It is true that walleyes are a lazy fish when it comes to feeding habits; you've got to lay a bait right in front of their noses, because they won't move very far to get it. But lazy swimmers? Jim Riis, a South Dakota fisheries biologist, can tell you how energetic walleyes can be. He's involved in an ongoing study on several Dakota reservoirs, and his objective is to establish daily and seasonal movement patterns of the fish. When asked if walleyes travel further than most fishermen might suspect, here's what he said:

"I'll give you three examples," he began. "On Lake Sharpe, we tracked one fish that swam four miles in eight hours, and another that went 70 miles in 25 days. And in Lake Oahe, a fish was caught 120 miles from its tagged site, two months later. Does that tell you something?"

And how! Why did these fish travel so far in a relatively short period of time? Were they isolated instances? Not according to other reports, including the Texas study. On Lake Meredith, radio-tagged fish were hardly territorial. Says technician Richard Eades, "Rarely was the same fish located in the same place more than once... it doesn't seem that walleyes have favorite spots that they would defend."

Could walleyes be more of a wanderlust species than we've given them credit for? We think so. If you've ever had good fishing on a particular reef or hump one day, only to return to it the next day and find it barren, you know what we're talking about. Walleyes may be lazy feeders but, as swimmers, they've got a lot of moxie. It pays to have a similar attitude when you decide to hunt them down. Too many fishermen die on yesterday's hotspot. Fishing memories is good for a starting point, but just because an area produced in the past, there's no guarantee it'll produce today. For bass, maybe. But not for walleyes.

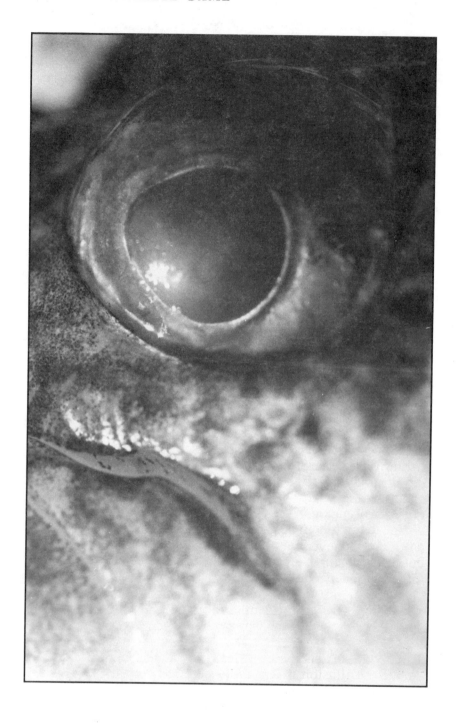

CHAPTER 4
THE TRUTH ABOUT WALL*EYES*

All it takes is one peek at a walleye's eerie peepers. There's something about those eyes that grabs our attention and holds it there. What makes them glow in the dark? Are they more sophisticated than those of most other fish? Unfortunately, over the years, some folks have gotten carried away with how a walleye's distinctive eyeballs function and how they might affect our fishing. Let's set the record straight.

Bright light hurts? "Walleye" is derived from an old Norse word that means having "a light beam in the eye." The fish's eye gathers more light than its prey—allowing it to see better under low-light conditions—due to unique reflective cells. That's why it shines back at you like a highway sign under a flashlight . This has led some folks to believe that walleyes are light sensitive, and that they "don't bite well under bright conditions." It is an exaggeration, to say the least.

Within the past 10 years alone, Mike has taken over 100 walleyes, eight pounds or better, from water less than three feet where he actually saw many fish hit his bait (or saw the fish before he has cast to them). Our biggest problem isn't light penetration, or fish not being in very shallow water. It's our *inability to fish them before we spook them.* To catch a shallow-water fish you must hurdle three obstacles: 1) You have to know he's there; 2) You must get into position for a good presentation; 3) Your bait must reach the fish before he detects your presence.

How many anglers stumble at the first one? If they don't think a walleye will ever be up that high because of his sensitive eyes, they'll never overcome the second requirement, let alone master the third. Believe us. Fish are there. Harsh light isn't the culprit. It's the shadow of your 16-foot boat (quite an imposing figure to a fish) that spooks them. Learn to fish the fish before you scare them, and you'll find how off-base the bright light / spooky walleyes myth really is.

Better at night? The problem with this fallacy is that it usually doesn't end here. It leads to other inventions that help create the illusion that walleyes are mystery fish with x-ray vision. That's why some fishermen believe we need to fish for them at night if we r-e-a-l-l-y want to catch trophy-sized specimens. Many respected fishing educators believe that truly large walleyes become strictly nocturnal. Our experiences don't support that belief, nor does the scientific record.

To be sure, we shouldn't minimize the protective nature of a good-sized walleye. It got big by avoiding the mistakes that other fish made on the way to someone's frying pan. However, large walleyes don't "bite better" at night, even in gin-clear lakes. But don't most anglers typically fare better on a clear lake after dark? Yes, unquestionably, but not because fish bite better then. It's because the tactics used on daytime walleyes are no match for wary fish in a transparent environment; our strategies simply need to be refined and re-evaluated.

As long as we're on the subject of night fishing, let's shed some light on another gray area. Radio telemetry conducted on Chautauqua Lake did find that peak periods of "activity" occurred at twilight (dawn and dusk) and at night. But researcher Einhouse was quick to point out that peak *feeding* and peak *activity* are not necessarily synonymous. Apparently, the fish move about more because they're not as efficient in the dark. But then, neither are fishermen very proficient without adequate light. When you put the two together—scattered walleyes and clumsy anglers—the conclusion is obvious: Nighttime fishing means a shot in the dark for Marble Eyes to a lot of folk.

Nevertheless, walleyes can be caught by the dozen at night, and big ones at that. It's an important subject, and we've covered it thoroughly in Chapter 18. But let's not lose sight of *why*. Simply stated, dark skies provide cover for fishermen, allowing them to approach the fish without first alerting them. Again, the rule of fishing fish before you spook them takes precedence over any would-be shortcut.

Murky water best? Walleyes do not prefer cloudy water any more than girl scouts prefer girl scout cookies. Although the two seem to go hand in hand, our on-the-water experiences don't agree with this popular notion. The reason for this idea, though, probably comes from the correct observation that the windy, dirty sector of a lake provides much better fishing than the calm, lee side. However, to say that walleyes choose milky water, given the opportunity, is giving them too much credit, and missing the mark by a mile. If that were the case, radio-tracking studies would bear it out. That's exactly what Texas biologist Joe Kraai *didn't* observe:

"We were surprised at how few locations we got from fish in the silty southwest end of Meredith," he said. "This portion of the lake is much darker than the east half, yet the fish spent almost all of their time in the clearer waters."

Clearly, (no pun intended) finding murky water is not an advantage—unless you find a good reason for the fish to be there. Waves is one (discussed fully in Chapter 9). Schools of forage fish is another. Walleyes can't see any better in most stained water than their prey, because their eyes—as marvelous as they may be—can't see through solid particles. And that's exactly what most murky water contains—clouds of suspended, solid particles.

The justification for taking note of those areas where the water is darker than other parts of a lake (or chain of lakes, or rivers) is yet another example of needing to be able to approach the fish before you spook them. So walleyes don't have x-ray vision; they can't see through objects any more than Mr. Magoo.

Color-selective? This is a subject that has generated much debate in recent years, and rightly so. If walleyes are color-conscious, fishermen would do well to take note. After reviewing reams of material on the topic, and comparing notes with the real world of successful walleye pros, we've concluded that the recent trend of colormania is little more than a fad. Experimenting with color to see what might be hot is one thing. Sticking to a particular color because that's the "easiest one for the fish to see at a given moment" is an entirely different matter. It's straining at gnats. Before we get so engrossed in such a "scientific approach", we should master the basics. Then and only then, we might want to take a harder look at how and when we decide to go with a specific color.

Our approach to color selection isn't earth-shattering. If we've caught several fish on a white jig, we'll go with the odds. Why switch, though, unless someone else is doubling your output? So be observant, and don't stay with one color because it was hot yesterday or a gizmo says it's supposed to be hot today. The acid test is what seems to be working *now*.

This is not to say that some colors aren't better for walleyes than others. We all have our favorites—ours is chartreuse—but you have to take a good look at Nature. Most baitfish walleye feed on come in shades of white, gray or silver so don't overdo it with other colors.

Recent research on this subject can be enlightening if you interpret it properly. Dr. Dwight Burkhardt, a University of Minnesota psychologist, investigated the walleye's eye with some rather sophisticated electronic equipment. He was able to measure the fish's micro-volt response to light, as well as examine the intricate makeup of its rods and cones. Here are some of his most relevant and intriguing finds:

1. In one experiment, Burkhardt exposed the walleye's cones (more below) to the bright beam of a laser; the cones gradually recovered their ability to generate electrical current to the brain, proving that the walleye should be capable of seeing *not only in dim light, but in very bright light* (emphasis mine).

2. Its eye is composed of two kinds of specialized cells, rods and cones. Rods are responsible for night vision, cones for distinguishing color and patterns. To have color vision, an organism must have at least two kinds of cones.

3. Of all living organisms, the walleye reportedly has the largest cones—about five times larger than a human's. And after studying hundreds of cones in the walleye's eye, two different types were found: one most sensitive to orange light, and another most sensitive to green light (orange-sensitive cones were larger and more abundant than green-sensitive ones).

4. Walleyes can obviously see color, but apparently not like human color vision; humans have three types of cones—those sensitive to blue, yellow and green hues. Therefore, a walleye can probably see orange and green quite well, but colors with blue in them look different than what we're accustomed to seeing.

Conclusion? Research somewhat parallels hard-core experience, but it's possible to overdo a good thing. Fluorescent orange and chartreuse have always been effective colors for walleyes (especially on jigs), particularly in darker water. Black has been a favorite in no-light situations. Solid orange or solid green crankbaits, on the other hand, aren't nearly as productive as silvers and golds with an added touch of fluorescent colors.

Here's an interesting experience with color worth pondering. One warm spring morning, Mike was fishing the Rainy River in northern Minnesota with Dave Walters, who is no slouch on walleyes. (Dave and his wife, Barb, are the most successful husband/wife team on the walleye circuit.) The two were discussing the merits of color selection and, to prove a point, Mike switched jigs every time he caught a fish. At one point, with five consecutive casts, Mike had five fish in the livewell; all came on a different-colored jig.

Solid chartreuse or solid fluorescent orange crankbaits are "too much of a good thing." Stick primarily with silvers and golds with a touch of fluorescents.

Walters still can't believe it. "Even though I saw it with my own eyes," Dave admits, "it's hard to convince others. Barb still doesn't believe me."

The question is, what if Mike hadn't changed jigs after catching each fish? It would have been easy to do what many of us do—prematurely conclude that the first color producing a fish is the "only" one to go with on a particular outing.

Line shy? What about fishing lines—can a walleye see them? Do some lines spook fish more than others? If they do, we'd like to know how. The main reason we fish with light line is because of the feeding nature of the fish, as discussed earlier. Otherwise, there's little sense to it, other than possibly adding better feel or more distance to casts, or maybe increasing crankbait depths.

Walleyes have a brain, and they can record experiences, but they do not reason. No, walleyes aren't instinctively afraid of line, nor are they intelligent enough to deduce that something dangerous might be attached to it. If they were, gill nets wouldn't have to be outlawed! This is just another walleye myth that keeps the walleye mystique alive.

Here's a case in point. Our good friend, Gary Grable, has refined a specific technique that involves line-watching with bright fluorescent line. Every time his partner, Mark Dorn, sees Gary haul out his rod and reel loaded with Golden Stren, he just rolls his eyes. But Grable catches many walleyes in very shallow water with the stuff. And if he can see the line, you know the fish can. Line color and line diameter in shallow water are less of a concern than how you approach the fish.

CHAPTER 5
HOOKING WALLEYES—THE FIRST TIME

One of the most frustrating experiences in all of fishing is losing a dandy fish—especially one you get a good look at—right next to the boat. Judging by all the big-fish-that-got-away stories, it must happen a lot . Everyone sympathizes with the fella who tells his hard-luck story, but it's no fun when it happens to you.

We think the problem is largely a correctable one. Part of the solution is exposing the myth that "small, itsy-bitsy hooks are best for walleye fishing with live bait." The theory is a shaky one from the ground up. It begins with the premise that walleyes need time to swallow a hook. You give them slack and hope they'll take the bait all the way down. Small hooks are necessary, of course, since they're more easily swallowed than larger ones.

If you agree with our thinking about how walleyes eat, then you know that the best way to catch one is to make sure your bait gets all the way into his mouth on his first attempt. If you don't, you're depending on luck. And that's what it usually takes for successful Lindy rigging—luck.

Although more walleyes have probably been caught with these live bait rigs than with any other kind of tactic, using a slip sinker to "feed" line to a walleye is far from foolproof. There are too many things that can go wrong, causing the fish to drop your offering.

Standard procedure is to fish a rig with the bail open on an open-faced reel and the line looped around an index finger. At the first sign of a strike, the angler is supposed to let go of the line, so the fish can "run with the bait." But how many times have you tried a hook-set with the gusto of a Mike Tyson uppercut, after watching a fish run with your crawler or leech, and ended up with nothing but air? (Some guys really go overboard with this and almost fall in the drink. It may look good on television, but it won't add more fish to the cooler.)

Why does Lindy rigging work sometimes and not others? Its number-one weakness is the fact that a walleye must turn in precisely the right direction to be able to take your bait, or he'll drop it and lose interest. You see, when the fish swims away with your offering, he'll feel some resistance, no matter how free it's coming off your reel spool. To the fish, it feels like the bait is pulling away, and all he's trying to do is avoid what's pulling on him. As long as this resistance continues, *a walleye will not open his mouth*, no matter what. And as long as his mouth is shut, you won't be able to hook him.

Now if he happens to turn in the "right" direction, as he makes his run directly away from you, the line will slacken and release its pressure on him. Then, and only then, will he open his mouth and inhale your baited hook. (If the line is positioned on the right side of his mouth, he would have to turn to the right; if it's on the left side, the fish would have to turn to the left.) It's so simple, yet few anglers recognize this. And when you consider all the variables—the line catching a rock or weed, the fish turning to the wrong side, the angler setting the hook too soon—this is hardly a percentage presentation. Yet many walleye anglers fish exclusively with this method.

If this is how you fish, then perhaps small, trout-sized hooks are best. Releasing fish unharmed, however, will remain a problem. Yes, you can cut the line but, no matter what you've been told, a hook down the throat of a walleye is a complication to be avoided at all costs. A better method, as alluded to earlier, is to use a live bait system that ensures the fish will get the hook, line and sinker where it belongs. (See Chapter 12, *The Ultimate Live Bait Rig.*)

Small hooks don't hook walleyes as well as larger ones. Small hooks pull loose too easily if the fish is allowed to wear a hole around the shank of the hook. That's why a big fish so often gets off, after thrashing on the surface an arm's length away from the landing net. Instead of small hooks, we prefer No. 1 or No. 2 Aberdeens. They have a wider hooking radius and they'll get a good bite into the bony mouth of a walleye.

Finally, a few comments are in order about the common expression of "setting the hook." Did you know that it's virtually impossible to set the hook in a walleye's mouth? Ever try to re-hook a fish for a picture? We have, and it's tough. Fact is, the fish sets the hook, and that's the secret to getting a good hook-set every time. Here's how it works.

Instead of visualizing a hook being driven into the lip of a walleye, as you ferociously raise your rod tip, picture this: You need to *move* the fish off the bottom with your rod sweep—get him excited enough to make him shake his head from side to side. As he does this, he'll open his mouth in an attempt to rid it of your strange, foreign object. It's these forceful, open-mouthed head shakes—not a macho rod sweep—that imbeds the hook barb beyond the outer tissue of the walleye's mouth.

This predicament is similar to your buddy holding onto a crankbait while you tug on the line. As long as he keeps a solid grip, he'll feel no pain. But the instant he releases his hold, the hooks will sting him. So it is with a walleye when he first grabs your bait.

It is so simple to hook a walleye, yet most walleye fishermen make the mistake of *lowering their rod too soon*. Even though they're careful to keep a tight line, they fail to realize that mono really stretches. It takes distance, not just force, to put enough pressure on a fish before he'll panic. You've got to hold your rod up high—stand up if you have to—until you feel those head shakes.

A proper hook-set might have filled these hands.

Incidentally, here's one of the best ways to tell how big a fish is: Wider head shakes mean longer rod tip movements. Small fish are shorter, and they'll jiggle your rod tip; a trophy fish will make it "throb."

It's also a good idea to carefully examine the barb of each hook. In these days of mass production, some hooks get through the assembly line without a barb. Others might even be too big, especially on some crankbaits; use a small pocket file and shave the barb down a hair, so it'll penetrate all the way in and hold fast.

Note the dark line running laterally along the fish's side. Exploring this organ could be the next frontier in walleye fishing.

CHAPTER 6
FISH SCENTS OR LATERAL LINE SENSE?

C ommercial fish scents. They've been getting a lot of ink lately, and the number of products on the shelves has ballooned from a small handful (mostly geared toward the catfish market) to over 150 different brands. Do they help increase the catch? Theory says they should: A fish's sense of smell is reportedly a thousand times that of a dog, which is a thousand times that of a human. How could they not work?

Quite frankly, our experiences with commercial scents have not been proportional to the claims advanced by many of the manufacturers. Bob Propst, who is a pioneer of many walleye tactics used today, recently fished an entire summer with a leading brand, matching it up with gasoline. His results? A dead-even tie.

Yet some highly respected guides we know swear by a particular product. Mark Martin, a full-time guide on Michigan's Muskegon Lake, is one. He does a lot of prospecting for trophy walleyes at night, and he feels scent can make a difference in the evening.

But the problem with fish scents, as we see it, isn't only how they're advertised (pay a big name in the business to endorse the product, and make provocative promises). It's mainly with the fishermen. They're continually looking for a magic bait, or a shortcut to success. And this, of course, is foolishness. Most fish come the old fashioned way: through knowledge and hard work. Again, it's majoring in minor matters.

There are three reasons why you shouldn't get too hepped up over fish scents. First, no one has learned how to bottle "the essence of life." Dried fish parts, or fish oil, or anise oil, aren't even close. If there is a legitimate place for scent in fishing for walleyes, it's the control of L-serine, an amino acid found concentrated mostly in human hands. Minute traces (parts per billion) have proven to be offensive to fish. L-serine, not motor oil, suntan lotion or even bug dope, could affect your fishing success. It's a wise practice to keep "on hand" a biodegradable soap (Lindy's No Scent or Dr. Juice's Hand & Lure Cleaner) for periodic cleansing.

Second, fish scents focus your attention in the wrong direction. They cannot overcome fishing in the wrong place or using the wrong method. If scents give you more confidence, fine. But don't forget that millions of fish are caught each year on artificials that have no scent whatsoever—proof that there's another principle in operation besides the olfactory sensory system of fish.

And third, fish may use their sense of smell to find food, but it does not appear to be the kind of stimulus that causes most gamefish to strike. There is another part of a fish's anatomy we should take a hard look at, and it could help solve many riddles. Color and scent have been beat to death, so what is it? We believe that the study of a fish's lateral line is the going to be the next frontier in the fishing world. It is the most dominant sensory organ of a fish, yet we know so little about it. And it could hold the key in answering the eternal question, "What makes a fish bite?"

What is the lateral line? It's an intricate band of nerve endings running along the side of a fish. When you fillet your catch, you can't miss it. There's a separation of the tissue (like the part of someone's hair), and the muscle next to the skin is darker. The information it sends to the fish's brain is a combination of hearing and feeling, only on a much more acute scale.

Fish with larger scales tend to have more sophisticated lateral lines than those with smaller ones, and walleyes are up there with the best. Each scale along the nerve band is hollow and its "canals" are filled with mucous. These are connected to tiny hair-like cilia, giving the fish an extraordinary connection to their environment.

How sensitive is this sense of hearing/feeling? One researcher, Joe Lindell, says that with this organ, fish can readily distinguish prey species from one another; as a minnow swims by, it gives off unique underwater vibrations that make it identifiable. Every aquatic creature has its own "signature," much like humans have a distinctive set of fingerprints.

This may help to explain why walleyes ignore some baits and key on others. For example, if you use a minnow that's common to the lake you're fishing, you are placing something in an environment that fits. It gives off a "natural" signature the fish are used to registering with their lateral line. Put on a different minnow, however, and the fish might ignore it completely, although it appears to look just as good on a hook to your eye.

Perhaps the most extreme example of how walleyes might zero in on a particular bait with their lateral line is during a mayfly hatch. Other proven methods usually fail at this time, because the fish are interested in only one frequency: that of a tiny mayfly.

Have you ever wondered why crawlers are so effective on walleyes? They're hardly a major component of a fish's normal diet; the first one he takes will probably be his last. Lateral line research might have the answer: The signature of a worm gently pulled through the water is remarkably close to that of a three-inch minnow. And worms present a bigger, easier-to-see target for lazy walleyes, so it's no wonder crawlers produce so well.

A similar phenomenon holds true with certain crankbaits. Why are some effective for other gamefish, but not on walleyes? Tight-vibrating bass plugs, as opposed to slower-wobbling, minnow-imitators, especially come to mind. The litmus test is whether or not they come close to approximating the signatures of familiar prey. If walleyes feed mainly on perch in Lake One, on shad in Lake Two, and on spottail shiners and smelt in Reservoir Three, it doesn't add up that one lure should be sufficient for handling all three. There are always local favorites, and with good reason.

Big walleyes are tougher to catch than smaller ones. Why? One reason is that their lateral line is bigger. They can detect underwater disturbances more efficiently and accurately than smaller fish; it's harder to fool them, because they have more weapons for both defense and offense. In stark contrast are newly hatched fry and young-of-the-year minnows. They're little more than a pair of eyes and an egg sack. Lacking this sensory system, minnows rely on sight and cover for safety; when they can't see, they feel safe and come out of hiding more readily.

The opposite is true for a large fish. He's not as interested in safety now that he's outgrown most of his enemies. Instead, he's looking for feeding efficiency. That's why specific spots associated with large rocks and banks attract the largest fish. And when a fish is caught out of that spot, another one will move in. What makes these areas so special?

According to Lindell, it has to do with the "echo effect." These places provide a better chance to pick up vibrations of passing prey, and any walleye selecting them will be a more efficient predator. How? The underwater disturbances will bounce off nearby objects from several directions. The fish can tell what direction his next meal is coming from quicker than if he was out in the open. This may be the primary reason why only certain parts of a reef (or point, or river pocket) consistently hold big fish, while adjacent areas yield smaller ones.

Naturally, fish will also settle in definite pockets because their feed may travel to them from several avenues. A swirling eddy is a literal conveyor belt. The lesson is obvious. Make note of those areas that have been good to you. Break them down on a micro scale, and put your bait *exactly* where it should go.

Understanding how a fish's lateral line works might also explain the "tough bite" that typically accompanies cold fronts. Lindell believes that atmospheric conditions heighten a fish's ability to receive information from his underwater environment; his lateral line is picking up more information—direction, distance, frequency—from oncoming lures and baits. Lindell likens the situation to that of a person entering a cave; hearing capabilities are greatly enhanced. On top of this, clearing skies increase visibility, and the two factors combine for optimum conditions for fish, not fishermen. And you know who usually wins the game when that happens.

By the way, not every walleye relies on its lateral line to the same degree. Fish in clear-water environments use their sight much more, and in some instances their lateral lines have somewhat atrophied. Fish in turbid waters, on the other hand, have well-developed lateral lines.

Finally, inconsistent results from *identical* baits might be attributed to lateral line principles. Have you noticed that of five (or 10 or 20) crankbaits, only one or two seem to catch fish consistently? Although they're all the same make, model, size and color, one ends up with the most tooth marks—even though all the lures seem to swim well—at least to your naked eye. Could it be that the "anointed one" gives off a frequency that's closer to what the fish want, because it swims truer to Nature's best?

This is no accident, nor does it have anything to do with superstition. We've noticed it and so have others. (Some jigs even seem to be hotter than their identical clones.) If you don't believe us, ask Gary Parsons, who shared 1988 MWC Team Of The Year honors with partner, Keith Kavajecz. He tells of a remarkable "real world" incident that is hard to explain away. It happened during a 1984 Sturgeon Bay, Wisconsin, tournament, where he and his boat partner took six fish the first day—not bad, considering that the other 80 boats combined for only 13 walleyes. What's most intriguing is *how* Parsons did it: with only one particular lure.

"I'll never forget that day," Parsons recalled. "It was an individual, total-weight tourney, and I got my three fish right away. I then gave the hot crankbait to my partner, Doug. He proceeded to catch the next three fish, while I caught nothing, even though I must have tried another three dozen cranks that were the same make, model and color."

Gary Parsons, left center, has a long history of experimenting with "anointed" crankbaits.

That's intriguing enough, but there's more. "The next morning, the same thing happened," Parsons said. "By 10 a.m. I had my three fish, again with the same lure, and I let Doug use it. He took one more fish before the boat traffic moved in and the fish turned off."

From repeated episodes like this, Parsons has learned to cull through his artificials carefully. About "two out of 12" will produce. The others he throws away! Parsons feels that this phenomenon can overrule the "color factor," and it must not be taken lightly.

The moral of the story? Pay attention. If one of your Shadlings or Rebels or Rapalas catches fish, take good care of it. See if you can tell why. And look for others that don't perform so well. You might have to fine-tune your crankbait tuning prowess. But chances are, the frequency of each crankbait is largely determined at the factory, and you can only do so much with each bait.

PART II, LOCATING FISH
(WHEN NOBODY ELSE CAN)

"This is Professor Quigley; I brought him along to interpret our new computer graph."

CHAPTER 7
FINDING WALLEYES—
ON PAPER AND ON THE WATER

Now that the walleye mystique has been unveiled and disrobed, we can get on with the business of finding and catching fish. To win the walleye game, you must know the rules and abide by them. The fish are the ultimate judges, and they will disqualify anyone who cheats or cuts any corners.

Since you can't catch a fish that isn't there, finding fish is critical. If you only have time to master one aspect of walleye fishing, this is the one to concentrate on. The fish are much more difficult to locate than catch.

LEGWORK

Suppose you'd like to plan a vacation around walleye activity. Where should you go? When? Start by doing your homework right. In late winter, when cabin fever is high, boating and sport shows squeeze a wealth of information together in one geographic location. It can be the quickest way to gather all the details you need to plan out your best trip ever. Here's how to avoid a bummer.

When you attend a sports show, you should have two things previously determined: Your particular region of interest—Canada, Great Lakes, a Western reservoir—and the specific dates of your vacation. Then talk to the folks at the booth and get addresses and phone numbers of relevant chambers, resorts, campgrounds, tackle shops and guides for the region. Make sure you get the scoop on *when* the best fishing occurs, and not some slow dates that are hard to pencil in. Some fisheries peak in May, some not till August. Your vacation should be arranged accordingly.

Once you've assembled these contacts, call the appropriate chamber, or tourism department, and a nearby tackle shop. Ask them both the same question: "Can you recommend a good guide?" Ideally, they'll mention the same individual(s). Also, double-check the peak fishing dates you're contemplating scheduling. Finally, call the guide with the highest marks, and ask him when he thinks the best fishing usually is. If his advice jibes with what the bait shop and chambers say, you'll know he is not trying to fill bogus dates on his calendar. And don't forget to ask where to get the best lake maps.

Now is the time to set dates and prices with the guide. Follow up with a deposit and get a confirmation. The best guides are often booked well in advance. This may all sound routine, but you don't want any surprises. All it takes is one foul-up, and you'll learn your lesson. The same goes for your boat and fishing equipment. You don't want to waste precious vacation time dinging around with a frayed transducer cable, a bum battery, or a faulty ignition system. You can handle routine maintenance, but these things can ruin a trip.

When you deal with a guide, tell him exactly what you're looking for: a day on the water to show you specific spots, and not a heavy stringer of fish. You can catch the fish yourself, but you want to be steered in the right direction, without spending too much time getting there.

Naturally, it's possible that the guide might not take you to his best spots. That's understandable. But if you've asked him when each one usually produces, with what lures and at what depths, you'll have little trouble finding his hotspots. Your map will indicate other areas on the lake with similar characteristics... get the picture?

Hiring a guide for a day is considered demeaning to some. To others, it's extravagant. But no matter how experienced you are with walleyes, on new waters there will always be a trial-and-error period awaiting you. It's going to take some time. Doesn't it seem odd to spend $150 on gas, $300 on lodging, and another $25 on bait, yet scrimp on a guide's fee? And when you consider the fact that he can literally add extra days to your vacation, an additional $75 is actually quite a savings!

ON LOCATION TACTICS

Most walleye fishermen rely on memories to find walleyes, and they do this to a fault. They check out an old spot, and if it doesn't produce, they'll head to another (linked to a positive memory, of course). If the fish don't bite in an hour or two, the fishing trip might come to an abrupt end, or at least be replaced by an afternoon siesta. But this should be just the beginning. Memories are only reminders that something once worked in a particular spot. *Forget memories quickly if they don't produce.* Go on to other ways of finding fish.

Dream trips don't just happen. They take lots of planning and legwork.

One of the easiest ways, is by letting others do it for you. Watch other boats. Observe carefully. Are they fishing a point with a sharp drop-off, or a flat? Notice the method(s) they're using. Are they vertical jigging or Lindy rigging? Most importantly, are they catching fish? Walleye fishermen are a good lot. If they're doing well, they usually don't mind sharing the secrets of their success. Don't be too proud or too shy to ask. All they can do is say "No."

We never hesitate to talk to other fishermen on a new lake, or even on a familiar one. And if someone asks us what's working, we're happy to oblige. That's part of the game. So don't think you have to know everything when you first hit the water. Conditions change, often by the moment. Why re-invent the wheel?

After this, a pattern or two should emerge. Now you're ready to try it out. Don't go fishing among the boats, though. Let them have their spot. They earned it. Instead, look for similar areas on the lake and hit them. If fish are going on one flat, they're probably going on another that's the same depth. Look at your lake map (hopefully, one with contours) and duplicate the pattern.

When you find some fish, you want to let them help you choose the best tactic to use on them. Which leads us to the next rule of the walleye game: *Fish location* (rock pile, flat, weedline) *always dictates tactics and presentation* (trolling, casting, vertical jigging). Although we all have our favorite ways to fish, don't let them become sacred cows and nullify this important canon. It will cost you fish.

A perfect illustration of this principle is an experience Mike had on South Dakota's Lake Oahe the day a cold front hit. The previous day, he had found plenty of hot fish scattered along points, and now they were bunched up in deeper water in small concentrations. They were cold fish, not interested in feeding at all, so Mike decided to go with vertical jigging—perfect for deep, negative fish. It would allow him to keep his offering right on the snouts of the fish until one took a fatal nip at his bait.

Occasionally, a fish would commit, and Mike would add another walleye to his livewell. Soon, three guys in a red boat noticed Mike's bent rod and trolled over within casting distance. As their lures passed through the relatively small strike zone, bingo! They hooked a fish. Being veteran fishermen, they turned their boat around for another pass.

"Get ready, now," one said. "We're coming to the spot." Bingo! Another fish hit, but they lost it at the boat. (Probably using small hooks...) So they made another turn, and the one fella warns again, "We're right over that spot."

This happened throughout the afternoon, with the red boat spending most of the time coming and going back and forth over the fish. Meanwhile, Mike stayed right on top of them with his bow-mounted Mercury Thruster. Guess who caught the most fish? Mike tossed back about 45, while the other boat landed four or five. At the landing they had a friendly chat with Mike. They couldn't understand why three men trolling couldn't catch as many walleyes as one guy staying basically in one spot.

The answer, of course, is walleye mathematics and another rule of the game: *Either you're fishing, or going fishing*. If you submit to the rule of letting fish location dictate your tactics and presentations, you'll be fishing more than the other guy who does it the other way around. Of the eight hours Mike was on the water, seven of them were spent fishing—with his bait where a fish could eat it. The guys in the red boat, however, only got about five minutes of actual fishing in. On a 10-minute troll, their lines penetrated the fish zone for only three or four seconds. The rest of the time they were merely going fishing.

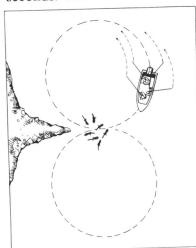

When fish are tight on deep structure, trolling isn't nearly as efficient as vertical jigging; on a typical 8-hour day, who'd get in the most fishing time? Who's fishing the most and who's going fishing?

You see, when you're re-baiting a jig, you're *going* fishing. When you're turning around to troll over a spot again, you're *going* fishing. When you're wetting a line where no fish are, you're *going* fishing.

The only time you're actually fishing is when a fish can eat your bait. Remember that. Let location dictate how you present your bait. The most successful walleye fisherman is like a baseball manager who plays the odds; bring in the lefty to face the left-handed batter, or bunt against a good pitcher. Sometimes it doesn't appear to make a difference, but in the long haul it will take trophies.

So once you've found fish, notice how they're located on (or near) structure. If they're tight to a rock pile or a break in the weedline, use a slow presentation that allows you to sit right over them; slip bobbers, vertical jigging or Lindy rigging might be appropriate. And if the fish are scattered—up and down a drop-off or along a reef or flat—go with a faster presentation that you can cover a lot of water in a short period of time. You need to do this to reach as many fish as possible. But the added bonus is that scattered fish are usually hot fish; they're searching for food, and they'll generally be more aggressive than bunched, cold fish.

CHAPTER 8
CALENDAR CONSIDERATIONS

I f there are no boats or guides to point you in the right direction, where do you start? Basically, only two factors affect a fish's location throughout the year: season and bait availability. But what about water temperature? Walleyes are not a temperature-oriented species, like trout or salmon, and it's usually a waste of time to be concerned with the thermocline (where water temps change most abruptly). Many windswept walleye waters don't develop a thermocline, anyway. The only time water temperature practically affects walleye location, is in the spring during the spawn and again for a short time in the fall during the mock-spawn. The rest of the year, the forage base moves the fish, not temperature.

SPRING

In the spring, ignoring water temperature can be a costly mistake. Since walleyes spawn in the same places every year, at predictable temperature levels, it is a simple matter to determine where the fish are at in their spawning cycle. You can tell by degrees if the fish are close to spawning (pre-spawn) in the middle of it, or finished (post-spawn). This, in turn, will give you a general idea of where the fish will be. It's not as complicated as some make it out to be.

Walleyes will move into their traditional spawning territories when the water temperature reaches the 40-degree mark. When it rises into the 42 to 45-degree range, the fish will drop and fertilize their eggs. And if the temperature has been closer to 50 for awhile, you can bet the fish are off the rocks. You can count on this, year in and year out. How this affects fish-finding is simple: To find fish, take a temperature reading. Few anglers take the time, but it can save a lot of guesswork.

All you need is a pocket thermometer, but a temperature probe, such as a Fish Hawk 520, is quicker and more responsive to subtle changes. Also, don't make the mistake of taking your readings on the surface during the day, where the sun can inflate your readings by as much as five or six degrees. The fish are down several feet, and a short-lived warming trend won't affect them. We hear of a lot of fishermen giving up after trying this method of locating spring walleyes because they don't find this method of locating spring walleyes because they don't find any correlation to where the fish show up and what the thermometer says. It can be traced back to incorrect temperature reading methods. So take your readings during the evening in at least five feet of water.

Naturally, the whole lake won't be the same temperature. Shallower portions—especially those with a southern exposure—warm up sooner than the rest; on large bodies of water, there can be a two-week difference between fish spawning in deeper areas and those in shallower ones.

Where will pre-spawn, spawning and post-spawn fish be? A tournament Mike and I fished on Lake McConaughy in 1988 is a good example of how these three stages affect fish location. This 35,000-acre reservoir is long and narrow, with a shallow inlet area and a deep zone at the base of the dam. Most of the bottom is sugar sand.

We had a pretty good idea of where the traditional spawning sites were: the rip rap at the face of the dam on the far east end, and a stretch of rocky shoreline further west. Walleyes prefer rubble (fist to football-sized rocks) and gravel to deposit their eggs, and they instinctively choose those areas that receive a steady wave action to keep them clean of siltation. Upon our arrival, we'd heard that the fish were "spawned out" on the west end, but when we checked the face of the dam, we got a 38-degree reading.

Our game plan was well-defined, but flexible. First, we'd hit the beach where we took second place with a double-limit the previous year. The females shouldn't be up on the rocks during the day, but the rocks could cough up enough two-pound males to get us in the money. Then, after we had enough fish in the livewell to place, we'd go out into deeper water and try to tempt a reluctant female that had only one thing on her mind: resting up for the spawn. From experience, we knew that these fish stage in deep water, adjacent to where they're going to spawn. In McConaughy, that meant Martin Bay or right in front of our rocky shoreline.

Again, the game plan was a sound one. It had worked before. But word had gotten out, and there were so many boats on "our" shoreline we could have walked across them. We caught enough fish in the traffic to pay for our entry fee and then some, but it would have been nice to have the fish to ourselves. That's tournament life.

Mike with a nice mess of fish taken in from 2 to 3 feet of water in Lake McConaughy.

Why didn't we fish the face of the dam? Only one reason, and this is a secret for early-season walleye fishing. The water was the coldest we'd found, and its fish weren't close to spawning yet. In fact, fisheries personnel gathered their quota of eggs there a week after we'd left. Don't misunderstand. There were plenty of fish there. We could see them on the sonar, hugging the bottom in 45 to 60 feet of water. But they were cold fish in cold water, not the least bit interested in feeding. We can always find some cold fish... but get them to bite?

You can't make walleyes bite, regardless of what anyone says. All you can do is be there with the right offering when they're ready to eat. But there's a better way, which leads us to the next rule in the walleye game: *Look for fish that want to bite, not those that might bite.* How can you tell? You can't always, but there are some guidelines.

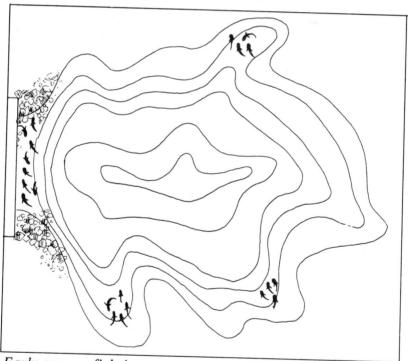

Early-season fish in reservoirs are most apt to bite in sun-splashed bays adjacent to spawning structure, or right on the rocks themselves.

For early-season fishing, the best method is with water temperature. Earlier, we discussed how walleyes eat, and how the metabolism of the fish affects their attitude. In the spring, colder water usually means colder fish. The spawn might have a mitigating effect on this rule, because it serves to concentrate fish; the more fish you have, the better your odds. You could get lucky. One might make a fatal mistake and pop your jig or crankbait. But generally, you want to look for warmer water where the fish are likely to be more active.

Better yet, look for forage activity in the shallows. Most of the food is going to be shallow, and a walleye that's in shallow water is there to eat, not rest. Deep water is usually for resting. If you train yourself to look for those conditions that activate baitfish in shallow water, you'll always be on top of walleyes, because they won't be far behind. In the following chapter, we'll discuss how to do just that.

By the way, if you're looking for a good walleye lake to fish the Opener (some states close the fishing season during the spawn, then reopen it) here's a tip. Don't mess around with cold-water fish if you can help it. We often hear the opposite counsel given in states such as Minnesota, Wisconsin and Michigan: pick a deep, cold-water lake for opening day, where spawning fish might be concentrated.

Baloney. It's like chasing the wind. You would have to be very good and very lucky to get into big spawning females. These are the toughest fish of all to catch. Besides, if you get lucky, what are you going to do with all the walleye eggs, make caviar? You'd be much better off picking a lake that warms up fast. Dark, shallow lakes with an east/west orientation would be a good bet. And those bass/panfish lakes receiving a decent dose of walleye fingerlings—especially the ones that get choked with weeds later on—would be even better. Leave the deeper, rocky lakes for midsummer.

There's another popular concept regarding spring walleyes that needs to be clarified—the so-called "post-spawn recuperative period." Speculation has it that the fish go off-feed for about 10 days following the spawn. They're supposed to be impossible to catch during that time, as they lie belly-to-bottom on the lake floor. Well, radio telemetry research does indicate that there is a recuperation period, but for whom? The fish, or us fishermen?

Texas Parks and Wildlife official, Richard Eades, did most of the tracking work on spring walleyes in Meredith Reservoir.

Bob Propst and a dandy stringer of spring walleyes.

When asked if there was a recuperation period, this is what he said:

"This is a tough question, but probably no. Walleyes moved considerable distances right after spawning, indicating they did not require any extended periods of rest."

Could this tough time period be caused by our inability to find walleyes, rather than by moody, uncooperative fish? Here's scientific evidence that does not support the presumption that fish ease into nearby deep water and go into a post-spawn blue funk. If fish are so burnt out from spawning, why do they travel "considerable distances" *away from the shallows?* Until we find research to the contrary, we're going to look for these fish whenever our temperature checks indicate they have finished spawning. We suggest you do the same. The fish go somewhere for 10 days, and someone's going to find them!

SUMMER

Early summer yields the best walleye fishing in many areas of the country for a variety of reasons. First off, young-of-the-year hatches of baitfish are too small for walleyes to eat. Second, the year-class from the previous spring is thinned out and relatively scarce. Third, because of this, walleyes spend 20 hours a day looking for food. And fourth, the year's new growth of vegetation hasn't cropped up yet, allowing fishermen to get a good crack at the fish. Put them all together and you've got a dynamite combination.

This is the best time of all to refine your presentations and bone up on your hooking techniques, as well as learn to use your electronics proficiently. Lots of active fish mean lots of opportunities. And don't forget the kids.

Where? Again, most feed is going to be on shallow-water food shelves. Fishing deep at this time of year can net you plenty of fish, but it's nothing compared to the shallows. Look for any extensive flat, reef, bar or point that's capable of housing baitfish; cover is the name of the game. Rock (broken and fractured, rather than smooth and round), weeds (preferably in association with other structure), and timber provide cover for both predators and prey.

This is elementary. You've heard a zillion times to look for structure.   But what if dense, prolific weed colonies invade the

Bass (above) aren't the only weed dwellers. The 28-inch walleye, below, fell for a strategically placed creature jig. Note the coontail.

scene, making normal trolling and casting presentations difficult? We've found a lot of fat walleyes living in downtown and
in the suburbs of Weed City, where few anglers knock at their
doors.

To mine walleye gold from the green stuff, you've got to
pick your weeds well. Not every weed patch will be festooned
with walleyes; weeds are weeds, but not all weeds are walleye
weeds.

On scattered weed clumps, it pays to check out which kind
of weed is present. Different species introduce their own obstacles and opportunities. Coontail, for example, has a bushy head
that gives the walleyes plenty of shade underneath. But its
stalks are thin and the fish have little trouble maneuvering
around to sneak up on unsuspecting perch and shiners. If the
water is clear, this translates into a fishery that peaks during
midday hours, when shadows are most pronounced, and again
at dawn and dusk.

Cabbage-weed beds are another good bet for midsummer
walleyes. They're a lot different from coontails. They have
broad leaves and a heavy stalk. A specific technique has been
developed for dealing with fish found skulking in these weeds.
It's known by two names: "weed ripping" or "creature fishing."
It involves cutting through the cabbage with a special type of
leadhead. We prefer other methods for rooting walleyes out of
heavy cover, and they are dealt with in subsequent text.

Midsummer can be productive, but you must pick your
chances judiciously. A fish that spent 20 hours filling its belly a
month ago, now only takes 20 minutes. So the secret to dead-
of-the-summer walleye success is timing. Besides the midday
peak in the thick of weed beds, be on the lookout for fisheries
that explode at twilight.

In some lake types, the best time to go walleye fishing is
neither day nor night. It's the short-lived, in-between-time of
twilight—that 20 to 45-minute period at dawn, and again at
dusk. Light intensity changes more rapidly at this time than at
any other, transforming walleyes from a mild-mannered Dr.
Jekyll to a wild-eyed Mr. Hyde in a moment's time.

Dick Ryder, an Ontario biologist, verified this by observing
fish in more than 100 Canadian lakes between 1962 and 1976.
His study was based on 1,000 hours of scuba diving and backed
up by some limited open-water angling. Don Einhouse's previ-
ously-cited study on Chautauqua Lake also documented the
twilight bite. Scientific data from both reports help solve nettle-

some questions that must be asked whenever the topic is raised. Like, "Why are some lakes better at these times than others?" and "What is better, dawn or dusk?"

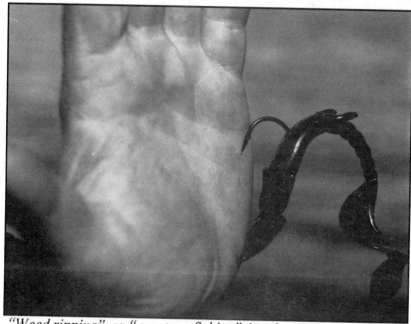

"Weed ripping" or "creature fishing" involves a unique jighead style; note the shovel-head design and rounded hook shank.

Walleyes are a remarkably adaptable species. What gives them such great flexibility is their eyesight. In the summer, their feeding levels are proportional to one thing: whether they can see *better* than their prey. Naturally, during bright daylight, both predator and prey can see well. But when light intensities begin to diminish, walleyes have a distinct advantage with their light-gathering tapetum, a reflective layer of pigment. On top of this, their prey becomes less skittish as daylight fades into dark, so they come out of hiding and begin to feed in the open on microscopic organisms. (You recall that baitfish rely almost exclusively on eyesight for feeding and safety.) Presto! Walleyes undergo a behavior transformation and go berserk!

Of course, you must be in position for this hot bite, because it doesn't last long. And you don't want to waste time on waters where there simply isn't a twilight bite. Turbid, bog-stained lakes are one. Here, walleyes can use their superior photopic (bright-light) vision to see better than their prey, and they feed very efficiently throughout the day; they have no need for short-but-concentrated feeding sprees.

But on clearer waters, especially those with a dense weed growth that provides cover for baitfish, now that's a different story. The fish have to load up while the food is on their plate before it disappears. And they do. So avoid dark-water lakes where you can't see a chartreuse jig deeper than four or five feet.

On some clear lakes, dawn is better than dusk, and on others the reverse is true. You need to experiment and find out if your favorite lake is an early-bird or an owl, because you certainly can't be both. After a weekend of hitting both periods, you'll go back to work on Monday looking like you did the previous Friday afternoon. Remember, this is supposed to be fun! The Chautauqua Lake study confirmed that one activity period was more intense than the other: of 45 complete 24-hour tracks, a full two-thirds of the fish preferred the twilight period of either dusk or dawn, not both.

Successful twilight fishing is strictly a matter of arithmetic. If your strategy is a good one, you'll get while the getting is good. If not, you could end up trying to scratch out a meal when

Successful twilight strategy is purely a matter of arithmetic; be sure to be in the right place at the right time!

the getting is probably gone. The key is knowing as many "food zones" ahead of time as possible. Anywhere that weeds don't grow—the tip of a point, a rock pile, an isolated hardpan—is ideal, as is a stair-step drop-off into deep water right at the weedline.

As is often the case with walleye hotspots, it is important to know these areas on a micro scale. Pick them apart during the day so you can work them over quickly and move on to the next one. And by all means, don't fall in love with a particular spot because you just caught a fish there. Fish should come fast. If the action slows down, zip over to the next spot.

Ironically, the best shorelines for good twilight fishing are often the calm, lee sides of the lake, not the windy ones. There's only one plausible explanation for this. On the windy shores, the fish probably filled their bellies during the day, when the surface turbulence reflected and refracted the sun's rays, thus giving the walleyes a sight advantage over their prey.

We used to think that the hardest thing about twilight walleye fishing was getting started. But now that we're into it, we realize we were wrong. It's quitting that takes self-control. Just when you think it's going to get better and better, it shuts off completely. So when the action dies, leave for home and rest up. If you don't, you could be too tired for the next twilight period. Then, it will finally dawn on you what this crazy fishery is all about.

FALL

As summer simmers down and fall blows in, windy conditions usually prevail. Big blows start banking the weeds up, and they really define the weedline. This can stack up walleyes on the outer ring, just like bass only a bit deeper. But as water temperatures drop into a certain magic mark, a unique fishing opportunity unfolds: Walleyes hit the shallows to feed again.

You've probably heard about those phenomenal fall stringers, the kind that adds a last-ditch spurt of activity in baitshops across the country. But, by the time you get on the water, it's over. You should have been there "last week." What gives?

Well, it's no hoax. And the snapshots in the baitshops aren't trick photography. In the spring, walleyes make a spawning run in shallow water, and in the fall they make a mock run. Except this time it's to eat, not spawn. For years, Mike had heard about the phenomenon. He used to vacation on Big

Stone Lake on the Minnesota/South Dakota border, and locals talked about the big October 8-10 feeding binge. One year he decided to make the fall flight, but the fishing was typical of most fall outings: cold and spotty.

On the last day of his trip, however, huge fish suddenly moved onto shallow, rocky points, and he caught one of the biggest mess of walleyes in his life. But after checking out all the variables, Mike noticed that the key wasn't a date on a calendar, but a *condition:* water temperature.

The same trick for finding spring fish—taking temperature readings in the shallows at night—works to a T in the fall, and not many walleye addicts know about it. To get in on the action, simply monitor the temperature *daily* on a local lake. When the thermometer slides from the 60s to the mid-50s, you must be ready to act. *It won't take long for it to fall into the magical 45 to 40-degree range that makes walleyes act out a simulated* spawning run. You must remember that water cools much faster than it warms; in the spring it might have taken two weeks for the water to change 10 degrees. In the fall it will only take a few days. Then, almost before it starts, the bite will be over.

Big deal, you say. Who can spare time in the fall to make water temperature checks, with ducks, grouse and deer hunting beckoning? Granted, it can be tricky, and it does take time. If it was so easy, everybody would be in on it. But there are a few things you can do to make life a bit easier on yourself.

October is a surprisingly good month for big walleyes.

For one, you could set up a buddy system and rotate the chores. Or, you could call area baitshops and ask them if any big fish are starting to show up. They'll know, and they'll be happy to tell you because it helps business (but don't expect to find out exactly where).

What good is such a short-lived pattern? Why not just fish deep, or at night? Hint: Do all lakes, reservoirs and rivers cool down at the same rates? Aha. If you see the big picture clearly, you know that this fall bonanza can be stretched out over a month-long period, in spite of its short duration on a particular water body. By starting with the one that cools first in the fall, and then switching over to the next one in line, and so on, it's possible to enjoy this "limited" fishery several times over on a variety of lakes.

Here's one game plan you could orchestrate. Begin with a shallow stream, and then move over to a small, shallow lake. Next, hit a small, deep lake. Finally, a larger, deep lake or a big

*Jeff with a nine-pound walleye and a bonus 20-pound pike.
And you don't think fall fishing is worth the effort??*

impoundment. There is a bonus here if you keep accurate records: Each successive fall season will be easier to time out, and a simple pattern will emerge telling you what to look for before it happens. What more could you want?

Where will the walleyes be? Right where you found them the previous spring: on rip rap at the face of a dam; river inlets; and rubble shorelines, particularly on the eastern shore of a natural lake.

Lastly, Mike and I have been investigating another fall pattern that's almost as exciting as the shallow-water pseudo-spawning run. It involves deeper fish in pre-spawn staging areas. We're not quite ready to publish the particulars, because we're not sure about a few remaining details. Look for this breakthrough in our sequel to this book. We'll keep you informed about its publication date.

PUTTING IT ALL TOGETHER

No doubt about it, seasons affect walleye behavior. Study the following charts carefully. There are some valuable insights to be gleaned here!

Rick Eades on the prowl again.

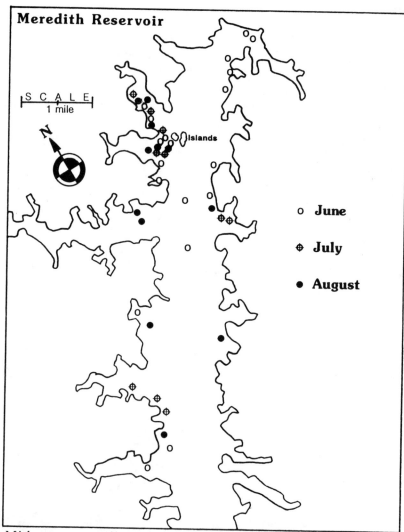

Mid-summer walleyes showed a definite preference for main lake points and islands. Also, flooded timber held a lot of fish.

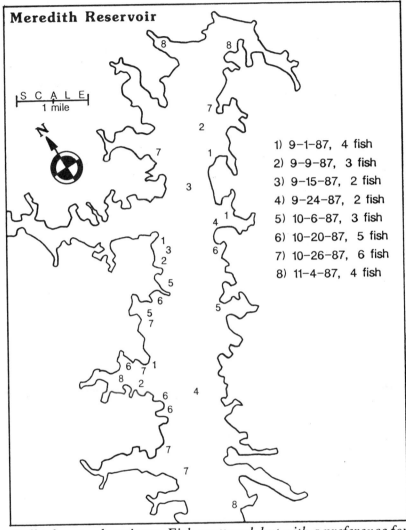

Fall telemetry locations: Fish scattered, but with a preference for the central portion of the reservoir.

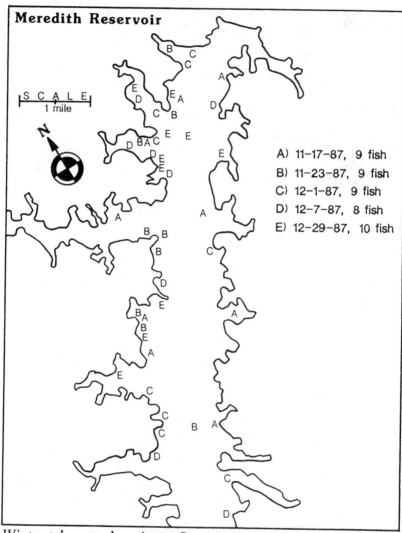

Meredith Reservoir

SCALE
1 mile

N

A) 11–17–87, 9 fish
B) 11–23–87, 9 fish
C) 12–1–87, 9 fish
D) 12–7–87, 8 fish
E) 12–29–87, 10 fish

Winter telemetry locations: Staging for spring spawn has begun with movement north toward the dam. Fish remained relatively scattered with both points and bays utilized.

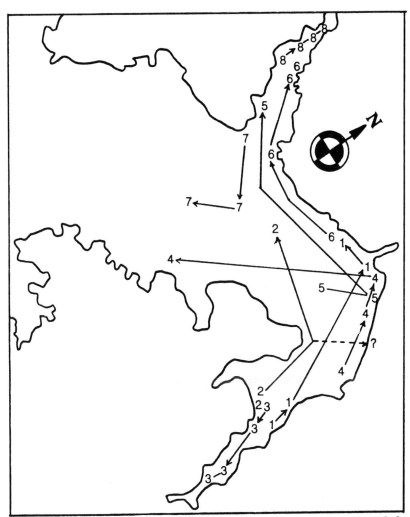

This chart shows walleye movement between 3 pm. on March 2, 1988, and 5 am. March 3, 1988. Eight fish were tracked and each located at approximate four-hour intervals. The numbers indicate the location of fish at those intervals, and the arrows show direction fish moved. Note: During a week of intensive tracking, the only significant activity observed was after sunset, lasting till about midnight.

CHAPTER 9
GETTING A VISUAL ON SHALLOW-WATER FISH

With these guidelines in mind, let's take a closer look at how to zero in on shallow-water walleyes. What we're looking for is a clue that might tip us off that some active fish might be close at hand. Ironically, other boats catching fish in deep water close by could be just the tip-off.

For example, any time we see fish coming out of 20 or 25 feet on a long, tapering point, we're very suspicious that some decent walleyes could be further up the point—as shallow as five, or three, or even two feet. If the boat traffic has confined its activity to the deeper water, we'll go right up and investigate.

Remember, the problem associated with walleyes in shallow water is that you can't see them ahead of time, because they'll spook out into deeper water. So just because you can't see them, doesn't mean they're not there. When your boat approaches, they forget about eating and head for cover; anything as imposing as your boat is big enough to eat them, and they always respect the size relationship between themselves and their environment.

Now this means that to find fish in the shallows, you might have to fish them. You can't cruise over them with your electronics or spot them with a pair of polarized sunglasses. Very long casts, hopefully with the wind, are the rule. An electric trolling motor also helps. The best way is with crankbaits, because you can retrieve them faster and thus cover a lot of ground.

But this still takes time. A lot of time. Here, we need as many shortcuts as possible. One trick Mike has pioneered for locating walleyes in new waters is "shining" with a spotlight at night. He knows that any fish he finds on shallow water structure at night will often use the same areas during the day (provided fishing pressure hasn't driven them off). Many fish will use the same rock of a rock pile, and all Mike has to do is remember where it is!

An added bonus of shining is eliminating unproductive water; if you don't find fish at night, you can forget about those areas for daytime fishing. Here's how to do it.

Wait for flat calm nights, so you can see the stab of light penetrating the water from your 200,000 candle power spotlight. Work over areas that looked promising earlier during the day. If a walleye is present, you 'll know it—his eyes will reflect back at you much like a deer on a highway at night. Make note of what the structure looked like and where the fish was in relation to everything. Was he on the very tip of the point, or was it below a big boulder? What was the exact depth? Any weeds? How many fish were there?

The next day, the same fish might not be there, but you've found a shallow-water target that feeding walleyes will favor. It could produce big fish for years to come. And once you put together 10 or 15 such spots, you can set up a sort of "milk run," and go from spot to spot. But remember, even though big fish are not always going to be on these spots, at least you know they have some potential. And if fish do show up, they'll be easy to catch, because they're there to eat.

A time-honored method for locating walleyes in shallow water is with visual aids. The best visual aid for shorelines is dark water, because it lets you get closer to the fish than normal. Plus, you can easily see it and key on it, knowing that any fish present are also probably there to eat. So if you see a bank with some dark water and some clear water, you know where to hit first.

Speaking of banks, we can take our process of elimination a step further. Ever wonder why those banks with a lip right at the shore, and not those that gradually rise up onto a tapering beach, hold almost all the fish? There's a very simple reason: Walleyes can corner baitfish by running them up to the edge of a blunt bank with a little drop-off, but they run out of water on the gently-sloping beaches, where minnows can swim to the safety of shallower water. This is the main reason why sand beaches are not very productive; the fish can't ambush as effectively, and when they do, they run out of water during the chase.

By "dark" water, we're talking about a section of a lake (due to iron, inlets, bog stain, soft bottom, lack of weeds that filter the water) or stretch of shoreline with less visibility to it. If you look closely, you'll notice that even small lakes exhibit variations in water clarity. A certain beach, for example, may be composed of gravel, and another one of silty loam. Guess which one will be darker, even without a wind?

Now dirty water is also a great visual aid, and it's probably our biggest ally for catching shallow-water fish. It's common fodder that the windy sectors of a lake kick out more fish than the lee sides, but why? An accurate understanding will lead to more fish in the boat, guaranteed.

Bob Palser with a hard-fought stringer of 6 to 10 pounders (before the days of catch and release). You can bank on big fish at the first lip when conditions are ripe.

Within minutes of waves silting up the beach, Bob netted this 10-pounder for Mike. The fish was released.

As waves pound the beach, they break up bottom sediment—sand, silt, organisms—and pull them up where they can be moved to other parts of the shore. At first, only concentrated areas cloud up but, as the process builds, the entire shoreline accumulates suspended particles. The width of the dirty water may vary from a few feet to several miles.

Now the reason wind-swept shorelines are so good to fishermen is simple: It's easier to get a bait in front of a fish without first being detected. We hate to sound like a broken record but, as you can see, this is a mighty important rule. Bob Propst has caught hundreds of walleyes while his outboard motor nearly hit bottom between the waves and his line was only 10 feet behind the boat. If he tried to do that on a calm sea, he'd be lucky to catch a bullhead.

Dirty water can be its own hotspot for two reasons. First, baitfish get confused and disoriented as they become dislodged from bottom hiding spaces. They feel safe, anyway, because their sight is their only warning system, and they can't see danger with all the suspended particles clouding their vision. Also, plankton is conveniently gathered up for them, so they remain in open water and feed.

And second, although walleyes can't see that well either, they "see" better. A walleye doesn't have x-ray vision to look through the particles, but he can use another sensory system, his lateral line, to determine the exact location of baitfish. Before it's too late, a walleye can ease closer and suck in the morsel. It's very easy for walleyes to fill up under these conditions.

Armed with this understanding, you'll want to capitalize quickly on the unfolding scenario—before it's too late. The secret to this fishery is *being there as it develops*, before the walleyes have eaten their fill. Sure, you can probably catch fish all day along the mudline, but it won't be nearly as fast and furious as the first 10 or 15 minutes.

Incidentally, for years, anglers have been told to "fish the mudlines." This is misleading. The break from dirty water to clear water is not necessarily where the fish will be. Rather, they will be where the drop-off is, or some other ambush point. Don't worry about where the edge of the dirty water is. The walleyes will be *in* the muddy water where they can launch a sneak attack, not necessarily on the edge of it.

An incident from the 1986 South Dakota Governor's Cup is a good illustration of how timing can affect mudline fishing. Mike and Bob were 20 miles up the lake on a dead calm day, an

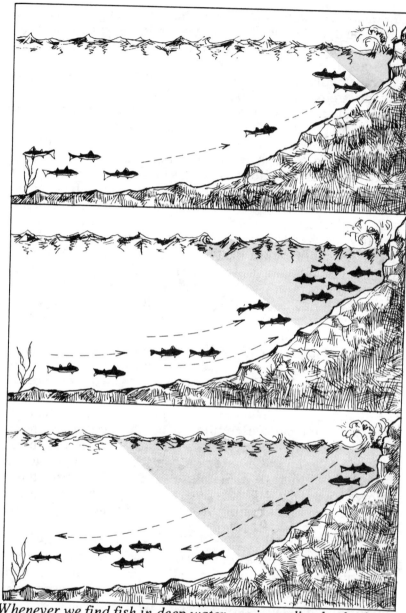

Whenever we find fish in deep water, we immediately check out the closest shallow-water structure. Hot fish will move up the water column quickly to feed, as wind and dirty water create cover. Be alert! Don't get there after the frenzy has subsided.

afternoon Dakota blow began to stir. First, tiny rings rippled across the huge reservoir. Before long, white caps were rolling out of the west, with shaving-cream foam piling up on the eastern shore.

Well before the first wave crested, Mike and Bob noticed that the breeze was picking up. They picked up, too. Mike just laughed at Bob as they headed for Okobojo Point. There had been big fish off the point, but they were deep and hard to catch. Once the waves chalked up the water, however, big fish were sure to pull up and begin to chow down.

On their first pass, Mike and Bob actually put on a little show for the other boats working the outer edge of the point. The duo landed a dozen fish, and ended that first pass with four rods going at once, all doubled over by stubborn, hungry walleyes. Every fish came very shallow—five feet or less. Meanwhile, nearby boaters gawked at the sudden turn of events from their position in 30 feet of water. This little tactic alone won the tournament for Mike and Bob, and they set a one-day weight record on the MWC tournament circuit. Not bad for 20 minutes worth of work.

A similar occurrence often takes place on natural lakes. Inlets that are quickly flooded from a sudden thunderstorm dump roily water into the lake, and the fish will move in and commit suicide. Some will even run up the stream, feeding voraciously along the way.

Waves without dirty water are like a blind date; you don't know what you're going to come up with, but at least you're not sitting home without any prospects. Waves distort your boat's image, add confusion, turbulence, noise and oxygen to the scene. They're a good combination, and walleyes often throw caution to the wind—literally. But you can't be as careless when the water is both dirty and wave-stricken. Again, make long casts, or troll in S-curves over the shallow, fish-holding structure.

There's one more visual aid for locating shallow-water walleyes, one that most anglers rarely consider: rod holders. If you survey the docks on a lake, and you see a lot of landing nets and rod holders, it's a pretty safe bet that there's a reason for it. Walleyes probably use that particular shoreline. Believe it or not, this is one of the first things we look for on an unfamiliar lake. It's a great clue to look closer for other clues.

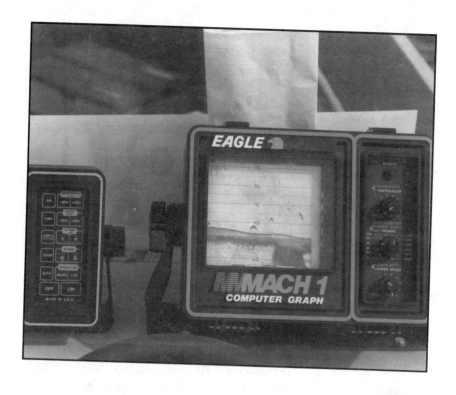

CHAPTER 10
ELECTRONICS FOR DEEP FISH

Without question, electronics are your ticket to deep-water fish. We're talking depths over 10 or 12 feet. Now, instead of relying on visual aids to find fish, we can see them on our sonar units before we wet a line. It must be emphasized that this is the best way to use sonar to its maximum potential. Most fishermen, however, stop short and look for fishy-looking structure, rather than for individual fish on the structure. It goes back to our first rule—you can't catch fish that aren't there. Usually, if we don't see fish on the flasher or graph, we won't wet a line. It's that important.

This can be exasperating, we know, especially for some walleye anglers who lack patience and confidence in their electronics. But it's the only way to go when you have fish in deep water.

Take a lesson from the 1985 North Dakota Governor's Cup, when Mike and Bob won it by adhering to this important principle.

Picture this. On the first day of the tournament, the guys caught a slug of fish on a particular point. Naturally, they returned—as did 20 other boats—on the second day, but they didn't fish it because their locater didn't light up with any marks on the screen. So instead of fishing memories, the duo left yesterday's hotspot behind and continued to look for fish. It paid off. Eventually they found an active school, and it only took 30 minutes to land enough poundage to place at the top.

Can you see yourself following suit, next time you're on the water? If not, read this next section carefully. It could make a big difference.

To begin with, you've got to have confidence in your sonar unit. You've got to know how to use it and how to read it. It's got to be properly installed and in good working order. Then, and only then, can you trust it. This is the number-one problem most walleye fishermen have with electronic equipment. They don't believe what it says, because they haven't taken the time to become intimate with it.

The antidote for electronicschizomania, however, doesn't have to be a season of Saturdays and Sundays staring bug-eyed at a CRT screen. There is a neat shortcut that can at least steer you in the right direction and perhaps save you many hours of frustration. Here's what to do.

Pick a *clear* lake with some weeds and underwater obstructions in it. If you have to drive 100 miles to find a body of water you can see bottom in 10 feet, do it. Next, run the sonar unit over rocks you can see, and note what the signal looks like. Then, run over mud with the same power level and compare notes. Finally, run over weeds and stumps. Again, look into the water and also see what it looks like on your sonar's screen. Experiment with the sensitivity button until you get the clearest picture. After this little exercise, next time out you'll be able to believe your unit.

Of course, the best flasher or graph isn't worth a dried leech if it isn't properly installed. We suggest you have an authorized marine dealer at least check out your layout. If one isn't available, here are six pointers that should alleviate 99 percent of your installation problems.

1) Opt for a wedge-shaped transducer for high-speed readouts. This is essential. And make sure it is positioned exactly the way the directions indicate (typically, on a slight angle below the hull on an aluminum transom; a dab of silicone between the hull and the facing of the transducer often helps).

2) If you do a lot of backtrolling, place the transducer on the left, or *port* side, of your outboard; you'll get far less interference because the motor's prop will be spinning in a counter-clockwise direction, forcing bubbles to the *right*, away from your transducer. Also, if you fish right-handed, you'll have pinpoint accuracy, because you'll be fishing directly over the transducer.

3) Never wire directly to a fuse panel. You could get spikes from other electronic equipment—CB, radio, Loran C, depth finders, etc. For optimum performance, wire straight to the battery.

4) Never intertwine electrical wires with your transducer cable. If you do, you'll be begging for interference. Instead, keep the transducer cable separate.

5) Don't bunch up extra transducer cable near the battery; keep the cable as far away as practical from your power source, and wind it in several loose bunches, rather than in one tight wad.

6) A transducer on a bow-mounted electric trolling motor is easy to rig, and is the ultimate weapon for precision fish-finding. Since the transducer moves with the shaft of the motor,

you can sweep the cone angle to the left or right and really scour a piece of structure on a micro level.

Say you've found a fish, you've just kicked the motor to the left, and the fish disappears from the screen. Then what? Well, you can safely assume that he's further to the right of the boat, and if you kick it to the right, he'll probably show up again. Can you think of a specific presentation where this would be most helpful? Right, vertical jigging!

Now that you know how to install sonar equipment properly, what kind of unit is best for walleye fishing? Is a paper graph worth the extra investment? Are flashers obsolete? Are liquid crystal recorders accurate enough?

Tough questions, but there are answers. Basically, each style depth-finder has its strong points and its fair share of weaknesses. Flashers, for example, can't be beat for two specific applications: trolling along sharp drop-offs (the extra-wide band says you're on the edge) and icefishing (LCRs can't take the cold, and graphs are too bulky). Flashers will also read a fish smack on the bottom and just outside the cone angle (more on this below), but they won't show fish between rocks on a typical North Country reef.

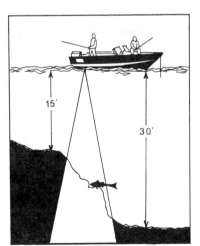 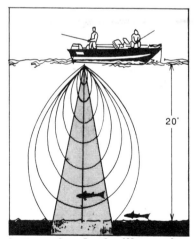

Flashers have their weaknesses and strengths. In the illustration on the left, the fish will be lost in the thick bottom line on your dial; the illustration on the the right shows a fish that is about to show up below the bottom signal—a nifty secret for finding fish on flats.

Graphs are better for revealing fish wedged in the rocks, and this feature alone has us persuaded that graphs are indispensable for fishing rocky natural lakes. They're also good for recording on paper what a particular reef or stretch of shoreline looks like. And nothing discriminates clumps of baitfish, small fish and larger ones from one another like a paper graph. But the cost, and the monkeying around with rolls of paper (that, by the way, are useless when wet) are strong deterrents to many anti-sonar anglers.

LCRs have been hailed lately as the answer for all our electronics needs. But they, too, have serious limitations. Present technology allows for 200 pixels (dots representing objects) vertically, such as Lowrance's LMS-300. Compare this to Eagle's Mach 1 paper graph of 500 pixels, and Lowrance's X-16, which has 1,000. It's obvious that the resolution, or detail, in an LCR is not sufficient for separating fish from the bottom, or deciphering a small school of baitfish from an individual fish.

So what's the answer, buy all three? Well, we do, but it's not necessary. If you keep in mind these and the following six tips, you can decide which unit is best for your particular style of fishing, as well as know how to optimize your opportunities with it:

1) Flashers are a great buy now, and anyone who lives in the snow belt should own one. They can take you out of the ice age and put you in the 20th century, where you belong. Icefishing without a flasher is like going golfing without a driver; you can still get to the green, but it won't be as much fun, and it will take a lot longer. Only, be sure to purchase a second transducer, in addition to the standard 20-degree model that's best suited for open-water applications. An eight or 10-degree transducer is perfect for reading signals through the ice.

2) Flashers can read fish on the outside edge of the cone angle and thus reveal fish that other units might miss. This is a little-known trick Mike uses to get into position and ready himself for a potential hit. The secret for finding these fish is to look for them on your flasher *below the bottom reading.* They appear to be below the bottom, because the portion of the signal reflecting off the fish has to travel farther than those signals bouncing off the bottom directly below the boat. This can be a tremendous asset for searching for scattered fish on flats and uniform humps and reefs. It will not work very well on rocky, undulating contours, however.

3) If you need bifocals, an LCR might be a wise investment, since the digital depth readout on most units is quite large and easily interpreted at a quick glance. And if you do much Great Lakes fishing, many of the newer units feature surface temperature readouts as well as a boat speed indicator.

4) To get the most out of your LCR, purchase one with a zoom feature. This will allow you to blow up the bottom segment of your screen—where most of the walleyes will be, anyway—and double the detail you'll get from the unit. Imperceptive, scattered dots on a full screen, when blown up, could materialize into a school of walleyes on a second, closer look.

5) Paper graphs yield the best detail but, unfortunately, most anglers fail to tap their full potential. Why? Too many fishermen become preoccupied with scrimping on paper, and they commonly run the paper speed on their graphs at or near the minimum setting. What's wrong with that? Nothing, if you don't care to know if a particular reef is holding hawg walleyes or just eaters. A graph can tell you in a moment's time, but the paper speed must be set close to the max. Because its resolution is so acute, a graph can accurately display fish sizes on paper, provided the interpreter has taken the time to "scale" the marks he gets at various depth settings. (The key is how thick, not how long, an arc is.) So don't be a paper miser, especially the first time you run over a reef or drop-off.

6) Many walleye fishermen complain that their graph won't print fish "as well as their buddy's." If the unit is properly installed, the culprit is usually one of two things. Either the suppression control is turned up too high (most of the time it should be set at zero), or the power isn't set high enough. Simply turn it up until you get a lot of clutter on the screen, and then back off as it starts to disappear. That's the correct setting. Then, if the unit still doesn't read any fish, there's only one thing left to do: switch lakes!

CONTOUR CUTTING

Sometimes visual aids can help to find fish, and sometimes they can't. Two such shortcuts we always look for are narrows and the longest point(s) reaching out to the center of the water body. These features constrict fish movement, and funnel them into a narrow band of water. Day in and day out, you'll find

*Mike watches his sonar as he cuts up and down structure,
looking for "the depth of the day."*

more fish moving through these areas than any others in a lake or reservoir.

A lake chart identifying reefs, humps and drop-offs is a type of visual aid for deep-water fish, too. These are pretty common starting points. But there are often little subtleties that point us to areas with *catchable* fish, areas overlooked by the novice and veteran alike. For starters, the bottom strength on our sonar screen often leads to fish that no map or local guide could tell us about.

For example, we always start by running half-throttle over any of the above-noted areas, but as we move from area to area, we won't always race full speed ahead. If the depth isn't out of sight (35 feet or less), we remain at half-throttle and watch the strength of our signal. If we notice a thin, weak bottom signal that suddenly gets heavier and brighter, we know that the bottom has changed from a soft one to a harder one. Bingo. We've got a perfect opportunity to swing back and really comb it over in search of anything that might hold fish—a small scattering of rocks, a little curve in the contours, maybe even an old river channel. Any change in the bottom, be it contours or content, can hold fish. And today's fishermen need to pay strict attention to this. Most of the obvious hotspots will have boats on them.

Once fish are located on structure, Mike has refined a specific approach for further narrowing the search down. It helps him zero in on the best depth to fish in the shortest period of time. Instead of picking a particular contour, say, 20 feet, and riding it out until he's convinced that it either holds fish or doesn't, Mike makes half-throttle runs *across* several contours at a time. As he does, he notes what depths seem to hold the most fish, and his process of elimination is much shorter.

Zig-zagging a reef, flat or extended point, is not only much quicker than checking out individual contours, one at a time, but it gives you the advantage of getting acquainted with the area. And doing it at half-throttle is much more efficient than eliminating water by trolling. Which leads to the all-important principle of finding walleyes in deep water: *Whenever possible, eliminate water quickly with your electronics, not with your fishing pole.*

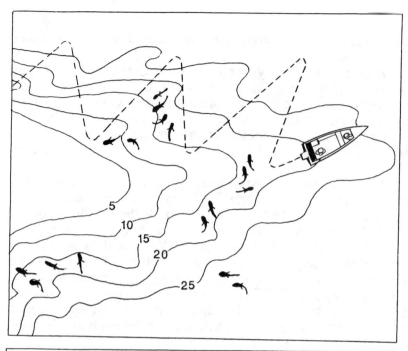

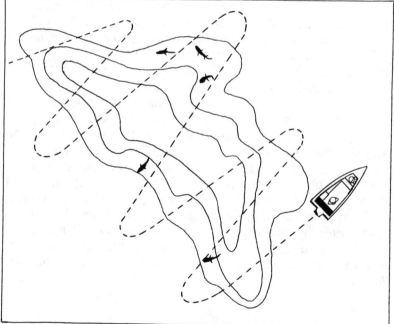

This is what contour-cutting looks like from an aerial view.

COLD FRONT WALLEYES

What walleye fisherman hasn't tangled with cold front fish and lost? They're tough, but we know a secret for finding them (catching them is another matter, though).   Over the years, we've noticed that active fish tend to occupy specific sectors of a piece of structure, while most inactive fish can be consistently found in other ones. It's no revelation that cold fronts tend to deactivate fish. It seems that fish go on the defensive, and eating is secondary to security. So the question of the hour is, "What does a defensive fish look for?"

The answer is cover. Yes, weeds, deep water and timber will hold more fish than the top of a reef or the tip of a point. But you'll have a hard time getting your offering into the lair of these fish. We know a better spot, one that's not only easier to fish, but one that usually holds walleyes that are a little more active: *cups*.

First, let's set the record straight and define terms. Some publications have used the term "inside turn," but it's a very misleading word with an equally misleading explanation. On a

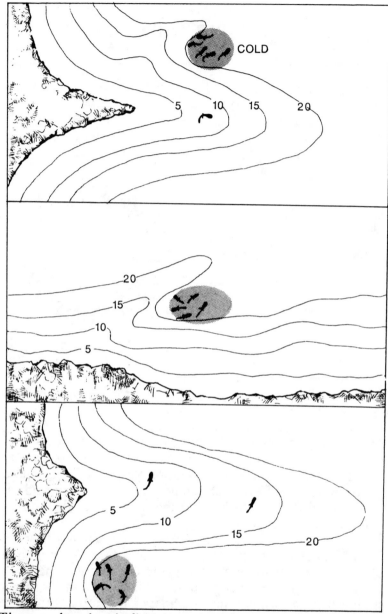

The top drawing indicates a cup above a point; the bottom drawing shows a cup next to shore below the point. The middle drawing is a representation of a cup not associated with a point. See why the term "inside turn" can be misleading?

typical point, we can tell an inside turn from an outside turn, but there are usually two of them—one on each side of the tip. We refer to them as cups, because they fill up with fish at certain times. What's so enchanting about the area where the point hits the shoreline? A cold front fish on the defensive perfectly illustrates the value of this little gem.

Hot fish will be on the very tip of a point because that's where all the life of a lake's system passes by. Obviously, any fish present are there to eat. In stark contrast, you'll find cold front fish in radically different places, where cover is available because the fish are on the defensive, not offensive. However, not all cold front fish are equally cold. Some are really frigid and a waste of time, while others are better described as being "lukewarm."

Cups are ideal cover for lukewarm walleyes. The fish need extra security and they get it from structure that's wrapped around them on three sides. To boot, baitfish usually aren't too far away, and if the opportunity presents itself...

But points aren't the only place to find cups. Wherever the bottom contours bend in and then out again, you've got an *underwater cup*. And fish could be stacked in tight. They're also good places for very large fish resting in neutral during non-cold front conditions. Flat calm seas, combined with gin-clear water and excessive boat traffic, could drive fish to various cups scattered throughout a lake or reservoir.

One way to find cups is with a hydrographic chart. The curves and bends in the contour lines indicate their location on the edges of points and reefs. However, there's usually too much slop in most maps, and you won't see many underwater cups on them. That leaves "contour-tracking."

Suppose you've just zig-zagged a reef, and the majority of fish appear to be in 17 feet of water. What you want to do is stick with that "depth of the day" and follow it wherever it takes you, instead of going where you know the reef is laid out. Eventually, this will lead you away from the structure, and on top of an underwater point. When the point curves back in again toward the main structure, you'll have found a precious cup that a majority of fishermen cruise right by. Remember its position, and come back whenever conditions put fish down and off-feed.

Incidentally, there's a similar shortcut for finding fish in reservoirs. Because water fluctuations on impoundments are common, a "magic depth" often prevails throughout the system as long as the water level remains constant. At the dock we hear

Cups fill up with some nice fish—even during cold fronts.

it all the time: "It was like magic. As long as we stayed in 22 feet, we caught fish. No other depth produced."

Translation? Wave action along the shoreline digs out stair-step drop-offs at the high-water mark. When the water line rises, a new stair-step will be created along the beach at the new high-water mark. Ditto when the water drops again. This pattern of changing water levels creates uniform drop-offs, where fish use them to ambush their prey. If conditions are right for baitfish on a certain shelf, rest assured walleyes will be slinking just below them along the drop-off. It's simple logic, not magic.

Do fish "choose" certain baits at certain times of the year, like a shopper at a supermarket? Read this section and find out.

CHAPTER 11
BOAT CONTROL & BOOT MANEUVERS

Once fish are located, it's critical that you consider how they're situated—whether they're scattered or holding tight. As we stated earlier, fish location (where) always dictates methods and presentation (precisely how). Put another way, it's best to fish certain ways for fish that are located in certain kinds of spots.

Fish that are scattered are likely to be hot fish, those that are looking for something to eat. There's a fish here, another 100 yards away. You want to choose a tactic (a method of presenting a bait or lure) that covers a lot of ground in a hurry; trolling crankbaits or drifting spinners behind a bottom bouncer would be two wise choices, because you can get your offering in front of more fish than with other tactics. Conversely, fish tight to structure are typically lukewarm or even cold fish; slip bobbers, s-l-o-w Lindy rigging or vertical jigging (in deep water) are best. You need longevity in your presentation for cold fish.

This is all bad news for the guy who likes to stick to only one tactic, such as trolling. He's going to run into quite a few snags, for example, when fish are bunched up in small quarters. As explained earlier, he'll spend far too much time repositioning his boat to get back into the fish zone. Again, we're either *going* fishing or actually fishing (presenting a bait so that a fish can eat it).

So letting fish location tell you how to fish is extremely important. As we have already seen from radio-tracking studies, walleyes are rather mobile and highly adaptable. On Monday, they could be scattered over a mud flat 22 feet down, and on Tuesday they could just as well be on top of a reef in two feet of water. With walleyes, your success is usually proportional to your versatility.

After the fish have been located, you've got to choose a tactic that will let you present your bait in such a manner that a fish can easily get it into its mouth. And you should do it with efficiency. So it's a four-step process: Location, tactics, presentation and efficiency. We've covered location. And we know how walleyes eat, which necessitates a neutrally-buoyant presentation most of the time. Now it's time to get fussy about how to present a bait to a walleye.

Boat control is considered a dry subject by many walleye fishermen. They treat it like college calculus, and would prefer to skip on to a more stimulating topic. Fact is, nothing could be more shipwrecking to a good overall walleye strategy than poor boat control.

You see, the demands of walleye fishing are distinctly unique, compared to other kinds of fishing. Bass, muskie, trout and panfish anglers, for example, routinely use their craft as a casting platform. Walleye anglers, on the other hand, typically present their bait *with their boat*. So good presentation is usually dependent upon good boat control, and you can't have one without the other. Therefore, as boring as it may sound, boat control is a key element to success, one that should not be taken lightly.

An illustration of underestimating the significance of boat control was etched firmly in my mind several years ago. It happened during a trip on Saganaga Lake, a large Minnesota/Ontario shield lake. For two days, the lake resembled a glass tabletop, and fishing was less than spectacular. But on the third day, the winds suddenly began to stir as I back-trolled a favorite rocky reef. My brother and I promptly hit a double.

"Boy, are we going to get revenge now," he said. "There isn't any place on earth I'd rather be."

Silently I agreed, as I back-wound line to a heavy fish. But I had that gnawing feeling it wasn't going to last long. And that which I feared came upon me: The wind grew so intense that I would have needed splash guards the size of a billboard to fend off the waves. And my cement block anchor—fine for "normal" conditions—just ticked over the top of the rocks as powerful gusts rocked my 16-foot Starcraft.

Everything I tried, including trolling into the wind, failed; the wind just grabbed the bow and swung it around at will, forcing me to increase the rpms on my motor which, in turn, ruined my presentation. We didn't catch another fish, yet we should have been able to fill the livewell. Oh, how I wish I could go back in time, knowing what I now know today.

And what is that? Simply enough strategies to tackle any situation and come out on top. The 1987 MWC Spring Valley Tournament on the Illinois River is one example of how boat control can make a big difference. Here, Mike and partner Bob Propst, finished second, twelve-hundredths of a pound behind Gary Roach and Randy Amenrud. It was boat control, pure and

First and second place, at the 1987 Spring Valley Tournament on the Illinois River, went to the two teams with the best boat control.

simple, that decided the contest. There were 80 boats in a block-long stretch working the best fish, which were lying in precisely 17 feet of water at the lip of a big hole. Problem was, besides the current, a stiff 50 mph wind made presenting a slow-drifting bait to pre-spawn fish very difficult.

Mike decided to face the wind and use his bow-mounted Thruster to hover or gently slip down current, while Gary back-trolled his 45-horse Mariner slow enough to do some slipping of his own. These men did well because they fished longer; they had a bait where a fish could eat it for a longer period of time than the rest of the boats. At the winners' table, no one could convince these guys that boat control is a boring subject!

All told, there are five kinds of boat control: drifting, back-trolling, bow-mounted electric trolling, forward trolling and anchoring. If you own a boat, you're probably familiar with some of these techniques. But there might be more to them than you think.

For example, there are three ways to drift for walleyes. First, you could motor upwind (or up-current) and let the forces of Nature push you across the fish. That's fine if they're scattered randomly and they're aggressive. But if they're on a particular contour that runs contrary to the wind or current, you'll need to do some "controlled drifting." One of the best ways to accomplish this is with sea anchors.

Sea anchors (a funnel-shaped, underwater wind sock) have been around for a long time, but when Bob Propst used one while fishing with Al Lindner, a large television crowd soon heard about them. Still, many newcomers to the walleye game have yet to give them a serious try. Whenever you've got a wind that messes up the direction of your drift, don't hesitate to tie one on. They've got several tow cords that allow you to position them upwind and away from the boat. And when you decide to pull up stakes, it's a simple matter to yank the cord that's attached to the small end of the funnel; up comes the rig without any drag.

Sea anchors will not only slow you down to a comfortable speed so you can present your bait properly, but they'll enable you to follow the contours on a long point where the wind is quartering against. The key is to reposition the sea anchor until it swings your boat around and the wind hits it "just right." Sometimes, two sea anchors are necessary. Just tinker with it until the boat swings in proper alignment to the shoreline or reef.

Sea anchors are easier to manipulate in a stiff wind than most anglers think.

And if you can't find sea anchors locally, you can jury-rig a pair of plastic five-gallon buckets on about a 10-foot rope.

Besides ordinary drifting and drifting with sea anchors, there's "power drifting." Sometimes even a pair of sea anchors won't be enough to correct the wind's direction to allow you to follow a piece of structure where you know the fish are concentrated. That's where the bow-mounted electric comes in. Walleye anglers are just beginning to discover that their bassin' cousins aren't the only ones who can benefit from this ingenious invention.

Bow mounts are perfect for keeping a drift properly lined up on a point, reef or weedline. All you have to do is give it a little juice when your sonar says you're sliding off the fish zone. It's a good way to get acquainted with the unit. It's also a good idea to use marker buoys to keep tabs on your position. Straying off the mark is easy to do on mud flats, large reefs and sweeping points.

Next in line is "backtrolling." Bob Propst also discovered this method of boat control many years ago. Others made it fashionable, but Bob actually perfected it. What makes it so effective is the fact that you're *pulling* the boat, not pushing it. This can make quite a difference if there's a wind. Why? Because on a forward troll, the wind will grab the bow of your boat, and you'll be constantly chasing it as you attempt to compensate. Pushing a boat on a windy day will never yield effective boat control. But pulling it might. To pull it off, there's only one requirement: You must be sitting on the "pivot point," where the transducer is also located.

A major weakness of backtrolling is getting dumped on by waves as they pound your transom. A good boat design will go a long way, but so will splash guards. One of the best we've seen is Wave Wackers, engineered by MWCer Bill Herrick (Herrick Enterprises, 4001 12th Ave. South, Mpls., MN 55407). The units are made of Lexan, a polycarbonate material that's both durable and lightweight.

For ultra-precision presentations, a bow-mounted electric can't be beat. As an example, if you want to work individual fish tight to a brush pile or a small hump, it's a simple matter to hover over it or weave in and out, because the front end of your boat will swing to the right or left easier than the back end.

Incidentally, the best sonar unit to follow specific under–water contours is a flasher. It reads a drop-off as a *wide band*, rather than a *straight line*, as is the case with an LCR or paper

Mike uses his bow-mounted electric to control a wind drift.

graph. You'll have no trouble, therefore, staying on the ledge where most active fish will be. Our two favorites are Lowrance's 2260 and 2330. They've been around for a long time and they've proved to be extremely reliable, bug-free units.

Although you gain precision with the bow-mounted electric, you do sacrifice power in a stiff wind. The resistance of the wind, coupled with waves occasionally pulling the motor out of the water, can be too much to cope with. What then? If the fish are bunched up along a certain contour or a particular depth, you must present your bait with the boat slowly and methodically, and doubling up with your outboard and electric is the best way to do it. On many occasions, Mike and Bob work together, with Bob running a small kicker at the stern, and Mike tapping the electric at the bow. Naturally, they'll both have their electronics on and will be discussing what they're seeing so they can synchronize their movements accordingly. It takes practice, but two partners coordinating in like fashion can really do a number on tight fish in big waves.

If the waves aren't over four, maybe 4 1/2 feet, Mike often performs this trick when he's alone. He'll simply run his out-board (a Merc 135) at the proper speed to combat the waves, while he moves the bow laterally with his electric Thruster for correct direction. This also takes a little practice, but it's not as difficult as it may sound. However, it helps to have a boat that's properly designed to be run from either the transom end or the bow. Starcraft's PM 180 is an ideal rig for doing just that. It was designed by Mike McClelland, Bob Propst and Jerry Anderson, three highly successful tournament anglers and full-time walleye guides.

Another option in windy conditions is forward-trolling. Crankbaits are ideal for this because they'll handle a faster speed, and if the fish are scattered over a large area, you'll also be playing the odds. But the difference between a correct trolling pattern and a mediocre one is the difference between going for a boat ride (going fishing) and actually fishing.

Remember the fish's world. Everything is neutrally-buoyant. If you troll in a perfectly straight line, how is a fish going to eat your crankbait? The tight line will not have much give to it. Unless the fish is unusually hot, it will probably just nip the tail end. On a lucky day, you'll catch one out of three such fish. On an unlucky day, you'll get one out of 10 (and you won't even feel the other nine). Chapter 14 goes into depth on this phenomenon, but here's a sneak preview:

Troll in S-curves. Since the fish are scattered, you're going to need to cover a lot of ground in a hurry, anyway. Also, the outside lines will tighten and speed up the bait, which could conceivably trigger that rare, aggressive fish into chasing the bait. It would be a bonus under most circumstances. But the real blessing of S-curve trolling occurs on inside lines, the ones that slow down and create slack line in the presentation. These will produce the most fish, simply because more fish can get them into their mouths.

Anchoring is a final method for boat control, and we must admit that we, like many walleye fishermen across the country, have overlooked its tremendous potential until recent years. Anchoring has become a favorite for presenting slip bobbers to walleyes that move up and down on rocky reefs when the feeding urge hits. Jerry Anderson must be credited for perfecting the art of anchoring, and he really taught us a thing or three.

In some waters, anchoring takes little forethought. If the bottom is soft, even a mushroom-shaped weight will hold. But if the bottom is hard—worse yet, hard and smooth—then what? You'll need to use an anchor that's designed to hold in not-so-sticky situations. On the surface, this doesn't sound like a very common problem that many walleye anglers will face. But it is! Here's why.

For effective reef presentations, you always want to work the *upwind* edge. Not only will 90 percent of the hot fish on the reef be stacked up here, but you'll have the distinct advantage of working *with* the wind. Most anglers seem to know this, but they still anchor somewhere *on* the reef. This causes six problems. 1) As you anchor, the boat will drift downwind, away from the hot fish. 2) This will spook some fish directly below the boat (probably hot ones). 3) To fish the up wind edge, you must cast your offering into the teeth of the wind. 4) Your range thus becomes limited. 5) Casting your bait off the hook happens regularly. 6) You'll end up fishing the top of the reef and the downwind side because it's easier.

The only answer is to anchor off the reef, up wind. Sounds simple, but if you don't have the proper equipment, forget it. Unfortunately, many reefs are surrounded by small pebbles, and most anchors simply will not hold on this type of bottom in a decent wind. To avoid the problem, consider purchasing a properly designed anchor. We've tried all kinds, and the best for tough conditions is a ringed, "fluke-type" design. A close

Jeff with his favorite style of anchor–ringed fluke.

second is a chain-style anchor. Tru Trac Industries, Inc. (P.O. Box 713, 902 Conrad Industrial Drive, Ludington, MI, 49431) makes both that are rugged and relatively inexpensive.

For most reef fishing in the Midwest, a 75-foot rope is sufficient. Soft nylon, by the way, is the best material. But for Lake Erie, or large impoundments, 150 feet of rope isn't too much. With a longer rope, you can really cover some ground.

Start by fishing the immediate area surrounding the boat on a short line. Then let out another 25 feet of line and fish the next swath. By the time you've got 75 feet of rope out, it's time to reposition it on the boat. Move it from the bow to the stern. Or from the starboard to the port side. This will cause the craft to swing into the wind, giving you a different area to work over each time.

For successful walleye fishermen, boat control is a far cry from going for a boat ride. Once you master these fundamentals, you'll increase your catch because you'll be able to fish longer—present your bait where a fish can eat it—than the guy whose boat is constantly jockeying in and out of position.

WHAT ABOUT CANOES?

Yes, canoes can be a crafty way to get a crack at walleyes, especially in situations where larger boats are impractical or powerless to penetrate cover and get through shallow water. Small rivers and backwater areas, isolated bays in fluctuating reservoirs, inside weed pockets on natural lakes, and water bodies lacking sufficient accesses are prime targets.

Problem is, few folks know how to maneuver a canoe, let alone paddle one and fish out of one at the same time. I guided the Boundary Waters Canoe Area Wilderness in my younger days, and I've learned some tricks for making the ordeal a painless one. Consider these tips:

• If you must deal with heavy winds, try anchoring. The principles outlined above also apply to canoe fishing, but you will not need a specially-designed anchor. Instead, a flat rock tied to a strong rope will hold a light canoe sufficiently.

• Drifting can best be accomplished by hanging five-gallon plastic buckets over the side to slow the craft down. The buckets become lightweight sea anchors, but are also handy items for carrying other equipment on portages, if need be.

• "Backpaddling" affords the best means of boat control out of a canoe. If you master this technique, you can troll a piece of structure as deftly as anyone with an electric trolling motor. And, it's a one-handed operation that frees your other hand for sensing bites and setting the hook. Here's how to backpaddle a canoe.

First, grip the paddle where the neck meets the blade. The actual stroke is a backward one, thrusting the canoe in reverse, very similar to backtrolling out of a square stern boat. Next, make short, even strokes parallel to the gunwale in unison with your partner. That's it. You'll be amazed at how much easier it is than normal two-handed paddling/trolling.

• You can fish solo out of a canoe if you balance the craft properly. Rather than placing one rock in the bow to hold it down, use two rocks up front and a third one in the middle. This will add the kind of stability you need for carefree, hard-core fishing.

WADING FOR WALLEYES

It doesn't matter if we're riding comfortably in a $7,000 deep-V boat, or strapped into a pair of $70 waders. Whatever it

takes to get a bait in front of a moody walleye, we'll do. And wading is definitely the way to go under some circumstances.

Any time fish are shallow, or close to the shoreline, you might be able to catch more of them by wading than with the fanciest boat decked out in all the latest electronic bells and whistles. On some rivers and fluctuating reservoirs, you can't even get a boat near the fish at various times of the year. Many spring and fall walleye fishermen, who are careful to fish the fish before they scare them, have learned this valuable lesson.

Anyone can wade in, toss a crankbait or jig out and catch a few walleyes. But to graduate to the ranks of an expert, a number of fine points must be addressed. The first is fish location.

The most common mistake is failing to capitalize on shallow fish close to the beach. Instead of stepping into the water right away, take a moment to analyze the situation. Is there a perceptible drop-off right at the water line? Are there any weeds, rocks or logs that could be holding fish tight to the bank? If so, try a few accurate underhanded flips from shore. Any fish this shallow is there to eat, and it would be a shame to blow your best opportunity on a hot fish that would be much easier to catch than one that's further from the shore.

Another mistake similar to the one above occurs on points. Although there could be hot fish right off the tip during oncoming winds, there could also be some active ones at the cup, where the point hits the shoreline. Hit the cup first, then the area in front and to both sides of the point.

The angle of your approach is another fine point in bank fishing that can make a big difference. Before I did any scuba diving, I used to think that walleyes faced outward, into the waves. It seemed logical, since this was the direction most of their food would be coming from. But after diving during a blustery July afternoon a few years ago with my cousin, I was proved wrong. Most of the fish we saw faced the shoreline, at the drop-off, which they appeared to be using as an ambush site. The remaining walleyes cruised parallel to the shore.

The implications are obvious. For one, casts made directly perpendicular to the shore will not catch the attention of as many fish as those made so that the fish can see (and feel with their lateral lines) longer. A crude analogy would be your trying to catch a ball that was thrown *from your back side,* rather than one that was thrown *toward* you, from the side or in front of you. Wading out and casting over one shoulder and then the

Casting rocky points from shore can pay "big dividends," as Mike's stringer shows.

next would accomplish this beautifully as well as add longevity to your presentation.

A hard-to-beat lure for this kind of fishing is a shallow-diving minnow-imitator. Mike prefers the Lindy Baitfish, and I usually opt for a No. 11 Rapala. If you wade to the edge of the drop-off and cast right on top of it, your entire retrieve is going to be in the strike zone; the crankbait will dive about three or four feet initially, and run at that depth for the duration of the retrieve. Again, you'll be playing the odds.

Now if you want to take it a step further, once you've worked a particular stretch of shoreline to your satisfaction, back out and walk up (or down) the shoreline exactly twice the casting distance from your exit point. This way you won't be overlapping any water. And by casting parallel to the shoreline, rather than perpendicular to it, you will have economized your efforts to a T.

Casting floating minnow-imitators, however, isn't easy if the wind is blowing in your face (which is ideal for concentrating hot fish near shore). Besides the difficulty in getting any distance to your cast, you must deal with the problem of snagging up. And these lures aren't cheap.

Take heart. There are two preventive measures that won't cost much money but will save a lot of lures. One is to crimp several tiny spit-shot on your line a few inches from the eye of the crankbait. Surprisingly, they won't hamper the delicate wobbling action of the minnow-imitator at all, and you'll be able to cast it like a bullet. More important, this will cause the tail of the bait to ride up and away from the bottom at the pause of the retrieve. It's nearly snagless. And by simply adding more lead, you can cover additional depths without having to buy a tackle box full of crankbaits designed for different depths.

Another provision for saving lures is to tote along a three-piece bamboo cane pole. It will double as a walking stick and triple as an extra fishing rod to reach from shore those small nooks and crannies that might best be fished vertically.

To recover a snagged lure with a cane pole, grab the line near your rod tip and pull it through the line guide at the tip of the cane pole (if yours doesn't have a line guide, be sure to add one). Then, extend the cane pole toward the snagged lure as you continue to pull on the taut line. It usually takes a couple of jiggles to free a lure with this method.

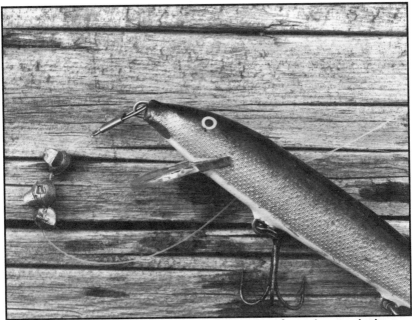

Crimping tiny split-shots near the nose of a minnow-imitator will keep its aft end riding up and away from rocks; also consider removing the front treble hook.

When wading in cold water, it's a good idea to wear a full-length flotation jacket; Stearns makes a dandy (Stearns Mfg. Co., Box 1498, St. Cloud, MN 56302). An unexpected dip in frigid water can snatch your breath away and sap your strength in a hurry.

If conditions are ripe, you won't be missing the boat by fishing for walleyes with waders. Keep these pointers in mind, but don't be surprised if you find yourself getting into wading over your head. It's as much fun as it is productive!

CHAPTER 12
LIVE BAIT & RIGGING

Under most circumstances, live bait will catch more walleyes than hardware. Most veteran anglers know this, but there are a lot of misunderstandings involved with the selection of bait. It's an overworked, over-exaggerated topic. Show us a walleye fisherman who doesn't subscribe to the "calendar of live bait" theory, and we'll show you someone who's going to win the walleye game more often than not.

By "calendar of live bait" we're talking about the notion that fish have a built-in calendar they go by when they "select" baits they'll bite on. So often you'll hear someone in the baitshop inquiring if the walleyes in Lake Smorgasbord are "biting on crawlers yet." The proprietor will often reply, "No, that doesn't happen there until the first week of June."

This is nonsense. Walleyes eat minnows year-round, and we can catch them year-round on crawlers, if we have to. A particular bait doesn't go into season because the fish chooses it. How many crawlers does the average walleye see in its lifetime? Not many. Then where does this concept come from? Certainly not from careful observations of fish.

You see, bait selection is strictly a matter of *convenience and availability*, not choice. For example, shiners are a great bait, but they're nearly impossible to keep alive in hot weather. Leeches, on the other hand, are a cinch to take care of when your shirt sticks to you, and you'd rather be sipping lemonade under a tree than going fishing. And crawlers are fine for in between weather. The question is, where are you going to find crawlers in February? Leeches in September?

If fishermen create the calendar of live bait (and not the fish) is there ever a time when one bait might be superior to another? You bet! Successful walleye fishing usually boils down to playing the odds, and there are definitely times when one bait beats the odds.

A perfect example of this is *casting*—tipped jigs, weight-forward spinners or even a bait below a bobber. You're going to catch more fish on night crawlers than with minnows. Simple arithmetic dictates so. You'll be getting in more fishing time, because every fourth cast or so you'll toss your minnow off. Meanwhile, that crawler will stay pinned to your hook much better, and you'll be fishing on every cast.

Figure it out: With an eight-hour day on the water, your fishing time will be 25 percent more with crawlers than with minnows. It seems inconsequential on the micro scale, but over the long run it really adds up. And when you consider short hits, there's a multiplying effect. Short hits will steal the minnow, but usually not your whole crawler; a minnowless retrieve is a waste of time, while your chewed up crawler could still catch an aggressive fish or two fish.

A good example of this principle is a joke Bob played on Mike a few years ago. The pair decided they had to learn how to fish slip bobbers if they were going to be successful on certain natural lakes. They were anchored off a rock pile, and were working the bugs out of this new system. Mike hadn't had a bite for a good 45 minutes, while Bob landed five or six real nice fish in a row.

"This slip-bobbering is definitely the way to go," Bob teased with a jolly, belly-shaking laugh.

"Hey, this isn't so funny." Mike said. "You're catching all the fish."

Bob decided enough was enough. "You'd catch fish, too, if you used some bait."

"What are you talking about?" Mike demanded.

"You mean you didn't see your minnow fly off on your original cast?"

This is as good a reason as you're going to find for not casting minnows. No matter how good your position is, what color you're using, or what kind of action you're getting, if you don't have a bait on, you're in trouble.

LEECHES

Suppose you've got the luxury of choosing from a list of baits. What's the best walleye-getter? Our favorite is leeches. They're tough, durable, and convenient. It has nothing to do with a walleye preferring leeches, you see. It's because a leech can be cast hard without being tossed off. And if pesky bait robbers (perch, white bass, panfish) are present, a leech in good condition will take a pounding and continue to swim for its life for hours on end. Ditto for short hits from lethargic walleyes.

Leeches are also a versatile bait. You can't beat them below a slip bobber. Even on a calm day, a leech fished in this manner can be effective because of its seductive side-winding action.

You can grow big leeches, but smaller ones in top condition will catch just as many trophies.

The only time leeches are tough to fish with is in very cold water; they become dormant and often curl up.

When stored in a refrigerator, leeches will keep through the summer. They will, however, shrink and begin to deteriorate if the water temperature is less than 41 degrees. If you're interested in growing healthy critters, consider the following advice from Hollie Collins, a biologist with the University of Minnesota who has studied leeches for a number of years:

"Temperature is the main concern," he maintains. "Between 50 and 57 degrees is ideal. They won't feed in water any colder, and if it's warmer, the added stress of reproduction will show up in their physical condition."

Some people like big leeches (we don't) and the best way to get jumbo leeches is to grow your own. What to feed leeches? Fish remains and meat scraps are adequate, but be sure to change their water as it clouds up—which could be daily .

Some words of wisdom to those new to leeches: Don't put them in your refrigerator without informing the boss of the refrigerator (whoever that may be). They give many folks the heebie-jeebies, even though the bait leech (*Nephelopsis obscura*) is not a blood sucker (*Haemopis*). Bait leeches are a scavenger and they do not have teeth!

Mike made this mistake when he bought his first pound of leeches. They were merrily swimming in a plastic bag when he put them in the refrigerator on top of a Tupperware bowl full of potato salad. When his seven-year-old daughter opened the door the next morning, she was confronted by an eerie sight at eye level. She "had nightmares for a week," and since then "leeches are not allowed on the premises" unless they're in Mike's boat stowed out of sight.

The best way to hook a leech is once, just behind the sucker. You won't hurt them this way, and you should get maximum action out of them. And when you fish a leech, it's best to think "slow." As a general rule, leeches seem to be more effective below a bobber or on a long leader and Lindy rigging (or bottom bouncing) in deep water. If you speed things up, then you might want to go with a crawler.

CRAWLERS

What can we say about nightcrawlers that hasn't already been said? Not a great deal. They're such a universal bait. But there are a few misconceptions we need to deal with, some that might ruffle the feathers of many experts. One is how to hook a crawler. In some parts of the country, it's sacrilegious to hook them any other way than with the hook barb buried in the very tip. That's one of the worst ways, when you stop and think about it.

If you're interested in increasing your hooking ratios, getting the hook all the way in the fish's mouth the first time, as discussed earlier, is the best way. However, this method of fishing crawlers (typically Lindy rigged) is going to guarantee short hits; the crawler's tail is as far from the hook barb as it can get. You want the opposite.

The answer is to hook your crawler in the middle, twice. By hooking it twice in the middle, you'll not only reduce the distance from the tail to the hook, but you'll create a presentation with more water resistance to it. This will make it easier for a walleye to suck it into its mouth because the crawler will grab more water as it is drawn toward the fish. It will go with the flow much more readily than a streamlined offering that's hooked at the tip.

Of course there will be skeptics. They'll try to tell you that a doubled up crawler looks "unnatural." Again, how many crawlers does the average walleye eat? Very few get washed in a river and even less in a lake or reservoir. Heck, crawlers don't swim like a snake or leech. If you want to get picky about it, it *is* "natural" for a crawler to be bunched up!

This same reasoning is used to argue against injecting air into the tail of a crawler. I used to inject all my crawlers underneath the ring, or collar. Experience has shown, however, that a shot of air in the tail works equally well. The main point here isn't where the air should be injected, but what happens (and what doesn't happen) when you do so.

At times, walleyes will suspend higher off a particular structure than at others. It's tempting to conclude that an inflated crawler slowly dragged on a long leader will be lifted well off the lake floor. It won't. This can occur only if you fish nearly vertically, and you repeatedly drop your rod tip and follow it back on a slack line as the boat moves forward. Why? As you troll, water flowing against your crawler will create enough resistance to push your rig back toward the bottom. It's next to impossible to get a live bait rig to troll more than eight inches off the bottom, without pausing during the trolling pattern. Only this will allow it to rise a bit off the bottom.

Another mistake crawler fishermen routinely make is not changing baits often enough during warm-water periods. When we fish shallow lakes or Lake Erie in mid-summer, we'll go through 10 times as many crawlers as we would in spring and fall. Don't go to the trouble of conditioning your crawlers if you're not going to check them within 15 minutes after they've been tossed overboard. Warm water will "dissolve" a lively crawler sooner than you think.

It's hard to beat a figure–eighting crawler, but you must take care of them if you expect to see healthy critters when you open that bait box.

Naturally, a fat 'n' sassy crawler is better than a wimpy one that's got the 4 o'clock droop. The key is temperature. Crawlers must be kept cool at all times. In warm weather, they'll literally wilt in front of your eyes. The best way to prevent this is to store them in a small cooler and put it into a larger one. Use plenty of ice.

If you blow it and your crawlers look like overcooked strands of spaghetti, take heart. There is a quick-fix method for conditioning crawlers, but it's a stopgap measure intended for short-term results. If they're not too far gone, place them on top of ice cubes (with an inch or less of water) in a cooler. Check them every few hours or so, and drain off any excess water. The worms should swell up and harden, and they won't drown as long as the water remains ice cold.

A better method for ensuring lively, figure-eighting crawlers is to grow your own in an environment that's both comfortable and nutritious. Until recently, that was nearly impossible. Now, there's a commercial worm bedding, Worm Paradise (H.T. Enterprises, P.O. Box 909, Campbellsport, WI 53010), that grows the meanest, toughest, healthiest crawlers we've ever seen.

MINNOWS

With the recent discovery of leeches, and the development of culturing nightcrawlers, minnows have lost their charm in much of walleyedom. If they weren't so fragile, they'd be the best bait of the three. Why? Because they have a natural appeal—the only kind that can actually trigger a response from a walleye. Let us explain.

Earlier we stated that it's not possible to make a walleye bite; all we can do is present a bait where the fish can easily get it into its mouth. But minnows can take us as close to triggering fish as we're going to get. Have you ever noticed your bobber suddenly twirl and jitter before it disappeared? Or have you ever felt a minnow on your jig dance a bit just before a hit? What's happening is something special: A minnow in distress will react in fear to an approaching predator. This reaction, in turn, often causes a walleye to react with a strike response.

So don't overlook minnows. They're number-one for vertical jigging, bobber fishing over the side of the boat, and during the spring and fall when they'll keep real well. Your main obstacle is finding the right kind of minnow. But our position is not what you're expecting to hear.

Some energetic fishing writers have gone into great detail on how this species of minnow is supposed to better than that one. We don't know about that. We've caught lots of fish on everything but sticklebacks, and it doesn't seem to matter that much if we're using a shiner or a chub. (Some go so far as to insist that male chubs are more productive than females, and others hold the opposite!) Granted, if a certain body of water is loaded with shiners, we'll try to find shiners. The lateral lines of the fish are used to registering that specific baitfish, and that all makes sense.

What seems to make a bigger difference, though, is the *size* of the minnow. And this is where many a walleye veteran stumbles. In fact, there is a commonly-held line of thinking that many fishermen follow about bait size that tells them to do the very opposite of what gets the attention of most fish!

Another eater for the livewell. Note the minnow bucket—an excellent way to keep minnows frisky during extended periods of travel.

The theory begins with the presumption that early-season fish "want small minnows." The reasoning is that cold water reduces the metabolism of the fish, and thus smaller meals are what they're after. Furthermore, summer fish supposedly become increasingly interested in larger prey as their metabolism kicks into high gear.

As logical as this may sound, it is the reverse of what is happening in Nature. Early in the year, walleyes are used to looking for adult minnows. At this time, new hatches of baitfish are too small for the fish to prey on. Only large minnows from the previous year are available. And in early summer—when most baitshops are well-stocked with large minnows—a new hatch of young-of-the-year minnows becomes abundant.

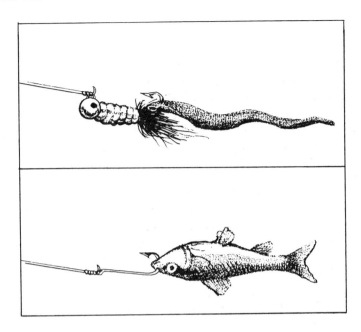

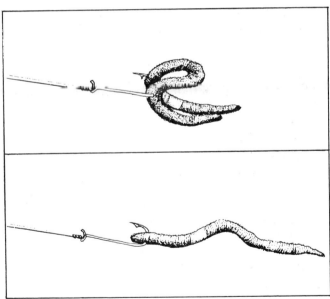

Proper bait hooking can be as important as how you present it. Leeches should be hooked just under the sucker; minnows always upside down; and crawlers bunched in the middle, unless fished on a crawler or spinner harness.

Your best strategy would be to offer what the fish are used to looking for: large minnows in spring and fall, and small ones in early summer. Every year, in June, we read in outdoor tabloids about the 10-year-old who catches a 10-pound walleye "by accident." Invariably, he'll be fishing for crappies with small crappie minnows. Believe us when we say it is no accident. Next time you catch a walleye, quickly examine its stomach contents, and see what size minnows are present. Then consider the time of year. This law of Nature is surprisingly constant.

What if the fish are keying on large minnows, and you can only buy medium-sized ones at the baitshop? Consider bulking up a jig with the dressing from a larger jig. We touched on this earlier, explaining that this will make the jig catch more water as a walleye inhales the bait. But this trick will also add mass to the offering, giving it the appearance and sound of a bigger bait.

THE ULTIMATE LIVE BAIT RIG

The main problem associated with fishing big baits is how to hook them up properly. Obviously, a big red-tail chub on a jig is not a high-percentage hooker of walleyes. It might pay in this instance to hesitate on the hook-set and pay line to the fish to give it more time. And sometimes walleyes bite so lightly that even panfish jigs won't get all the way into their mouths. For tough situations like these, only a neutrally-buoyant live bait rig that goes easily with the flow of water, or a coiled leader will produce fish.

How can a rig be neutrally-buoyant? What's a coiled leader? Answers to these and related questions might revolutionize the way you fish live bait rigs for walleyes. Previously, we discussed the main weakness of the slip-sinker system of live bait rigging (most commonly referred to as Lindy rigging); the fish has to turn at just the right angle to release tension on the line, before he'll open his mouth and attempt to swallow the bait.

Now suppose you could fish with a system that has some built-in give, or slack, to it? Would the fish instinctively "hold on" at the initial hit? Usually not. Your offering should flow naturally into the fish's mouth the first time. To best accomplish this, your live bait rig must have some slack between the weight and the bait. One method is with styrofoam Lindy snell floats. By positioning the float a quarter of the way from the bait, a slight triangle is formed in your line. On a five or six-foot leader this works fairly well.

Merely adding a Lindy snell float to your leader isn't enough, however. If you continue to use standard slip sinkers—foot, egg or bell-shaped—it won't be nearly as effective. The main job of a sinker is to keep your offering at or near the bottom without getting hung up. But one particular style of sinkers adds a bonus: It creates slack in the presentation from time to time.

Of course, we're talking about our favorite, the amazing Missouri River bottom bouncer. Unique in the world of lead sinkers, a bottom bouncer is basically a 10-inch wire feeler, with the lead weight molded onto the shaft, about halfway up. It's as snag-free as you're going to find, and when it bumps against a bottom obstruction, it "sticks" momentarily before riding over it. This inherent stop-and-go action creates slack in your presentation. Hence, a bottom bouncer does a lot of things right for you, without requiring any finesse to fish it.

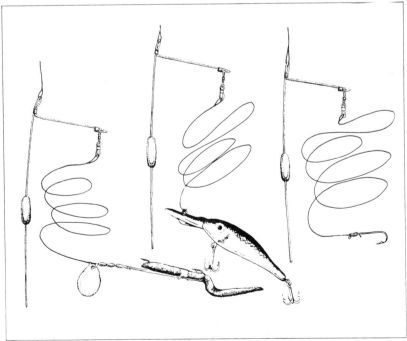

The bottom bouncer is so dang versatile. Ask Steve Fellegy.

Bottom bouncers are just catching on in most areas of the country, although backyard tinkerers have been using them for some time on several reservoir systems along the Missouri River. You may have a difficult time finding them locally. However, the Lindy-Little Joe Tackle Company (P.O. Box C, Brainerd, MN 56401) markets and distributes nation-wide their excellent Bottom Cruiser, which was designed by Mike and Bob. The Bottom Cruiser is an improvement over the generic model (which swings around in a stiff wind, causing line tangles just as you lower it into the water), so check it out.

We must warn you, though. At first, you're not going to be impressed with it. The first time Mike and Bob fished a Minnesota walleye tournament, held on Mille Lacs lake, they nearly got laughed off the lake because of their bottom bouncers. You have to realize that Mille Lacs is the geographic center and headquarters of where most of our walleye knowledge used to come from.

One sweltering July day, several local guides, including Steve Fellegy, were inspecting Bob Propst's boat. It was tied to a dock while Mike and Bob went ashore to get some pop. Mike beat Bob back to the dock and noticed that Fellegy had the locals in stitches.

"What's so funny?" Mike asked.

"What's that hanging on your rod?" Steve answered with a question.

Mike thought he was being put on. "You know," he said. "It's a bottom bouncer."

"What's it for?" Steve persisted.

"For catching walleyes," Mike responded. "What else?"

"Our walleyes are too sophisticated for something like that," Steve said, his buddies bellowing all the more.

That was a while ago, and it looks as if Mike might have gotten the last laugh. If you were to look in Fellegy's tackle box today, you'd find plenty of bottom bouncers. Over the past couple of years, Fellegy has fished a number of tournaments on the MWC circuit and he's found out how versatile the bottom bouncer really is. Granted, it may not be the best way to fish the mud flats on Mille Lacs. But on small rock piles there, it's hard to beat.

What makes the bottom bouncer a winner is its versatility. Mike fishes walleyes at least 15 different ways but, if he was forced to use only one, he'd take the bottom bouncer and a plain hook with a bait. With this arrangement, he can follow any

Bottom bouncers excel with spinner rigs.

structure up and down the breaks without snagging up. The bottom end of the sinker is only 1/32 of an inch in diameter, and it doesn't wedge between rocks like other sinkers do.

The best way to work live bait behind a bottom bouncer is by maintaining an approximate 45 degree angle with your line. Don't let your drift or troll take you any faster. For cold fish that need longevity in your presentation (a bait dangling in front of them for long periods), you can yo-yo a bottom bouncer s-l-o-w-l-y. Put your motor in neutral occasionally, and drop your rod tip back on a slack line. This often works for stubborn fish when a standard troll with a Lindy rig might not.

Of course, you can fish live bait fairly fast with a bottom bouncer, as well. That's when you might want to go to spinner harnesses—a single hook for leeches, a double for minnows and three snelled in tandem for crawlers. If you tie your own, be sure to leave plenty of space between the hooks for rigging crawlers; you don't want to bunch up a crawler on a spinner harness because it will create too much water resistance.

If you're not going to be trolling fast enough to make the blades spin, don't use spinners. They become a negative when they're not spinning, because they add extra weight and little else. Spinner blades also tend to wedge (in)conveniently between rocks. For this reason, top anglers like Gary Parsons never use spinners larger than his little fingernail. Even when the big Colorado or Indiana blades are working, he feels he can catch just as many fish with miniature-sized blades.

A bottom bouncer excels in a number of unique applications. One is fishing with kids. Will it ever save you the migraines! It's a very safe presentation. Just lower it to the bottom and let the kid hang on. It won't be long before his concentration wanes. He might even prefer digging around in the crawlers or leeches. That's okay. When a fish hits, it will usually have hooked itself without the customary ordeal of having to play cat-and-mouse with it (as is the case with most Lindy rigging). Only, be sure there's a rod holder nearby.

Which leads to another application ripe for bottom bouncing: "secondary rods." Many states allow multiple lines. Wisconsin, for example, allows three. Next time, try drifting a bottom bouncer with a minnow, leech or crawler with a *long* rod on the opposite side of your boat. You'll have increased your odds dramatically by covering a wider swath, and the rod (in a rod holder) is pretty much maintenance-free.

Kids and bottom bouncers go together like peanut butter and jelly.

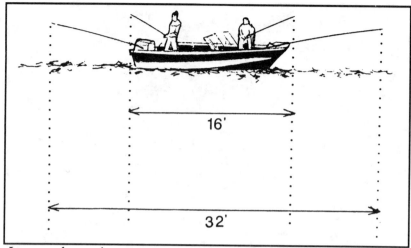

16'

32'

Long rods can increase your coverage by 100 per cent if you use them correctly.

Coiled leaders are another trick you can pull on ultra-cold fish when you don't want a fish to run with the bait and hope he'll swallow it. A coiled leader is a sneaky invention of Mike's. It's merely a section of old line from a fishing reel. When it comes off the spool, it comes out in coils with a lot of memory to it. This memory straightens out easily when a fish hits your bait, no matter how lightly. We like to call them "memory leaders" because we have a lot of fond memories tied to them.

One such memory is the 1985 Mercury National, held on Wisconsin's Lake Winnebago, near Oshkosh. Mike was leading the tournament after the first day of the two-day contest, but on the second day a big wind whipped up. His fish moved, and he was having trouble locating others. Finally, he found some in a six-foot diameter pocket, off a tiny underwater point in a foot of water. But they were so dormant, he got nothing but short hits; after going all day without a touch, he missed three fish in a row.

He decided to lighten up his line to cut down on the water resistance. This should allow his quarter-ounce jig (the wind made anything lighter unmanageable) to make it into the mouth of the lethargic fish. It worked—almost. After going from six pound down to two pound mono, he hooked the next three fish, but they all broke off! They were too active once hooked.

By now Mike's heart was really pounding. He'd found the fish. All he had to do was get them in the boat. That's when he realized that he was pumped up and not thinking. After he analyzed the situation, he quickly concluded that a memory leader would be the only way the fish would get the hook in their mouths; the wind was blowing his line sideways and taking all the slack out of it, even on the drop of the jig.

After tying a fine diameter, Aberdeen hook on a three-foot section of old 10-pound mono, Mike's "luck" changed. He caught the next seven fish that hit. And he won the tournament, all because of a kinky leader system.

Jerome Robinson, noted outdoor writer with *Sports Afield,* flew to South Dakota to investigate the possibilities of this strange, new fishing system. He wanted to see if it would work for other systems, so he fished trout in some stock dams. His presentation was a minnow and a couple of split-shot below a standard bobber. The first six hits produced nary a trout. But after rigging up a memory leader, Robinson turned the tables on the fish and caught the next six in a row. That's how effective a memory leader can be; it just lets the offering go with the flow of water, into the fish's mouth.

Coiled leaders should be tried when all else fails. Often they won't. Photo by Jerome Robinson.

Memory leaders are hardly a panacea. They're temperamental to fish with, and it takes a certain commitment to stick with them. For example, after you've caught a fish, you'll have to take the old leader off and tie up another one; the memory will have been stretched out by the weight of the fish. The same goes with a snag. You'll have to retie again.

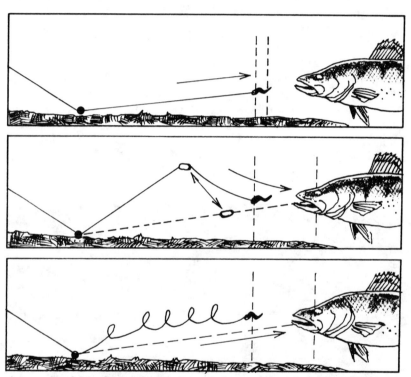

A standard Lindy rig (top) doesn't have enough "play" between the weight and the bait; floats (center) and coiled leaders (bottom) certainly do.

And even if you haven't caught a fish or snagged up, within an hour or so you'll still have to re-rig. Just using it will cause it to lose its memory after a short while. So you'll have to ask yourself, "Is it worth the time invested to go to all this bother?" If the fish are really cold, and you know you've missed some very faint hits, perhaps it is.

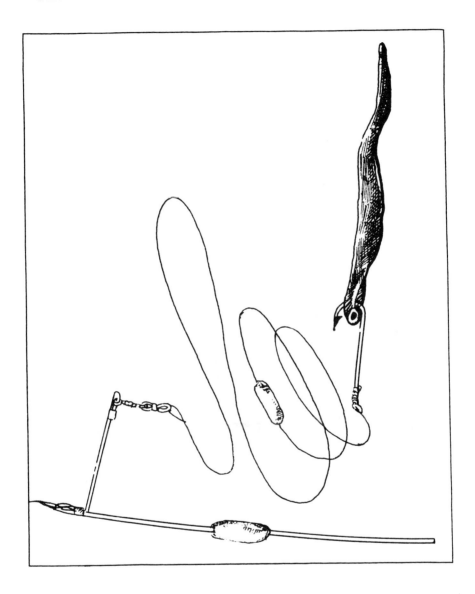

CHAPTER 13
JIGFISHING

Nothing separates a good walleye fisherman from an average one more graphically than jigging. Besides the fundamentals of choosing the right line to go with the right jig weight (the lighter for both, the better) attitude and concentration will make or break you.

We suggest that you make your attitude adjustment right now and quit trying to make a fish strike your jig. Instead, begin to develop an attitude of keeping in contact with the bottom. This will ensure maximum "fall time," in as near a vertical position as possible and allow the fish to eat your jig. You want to maintain a presentation that's close to the structure, where the fish are most likely to be lurking, rather than one that drags through it. Generally, you'll catch just as many fish with half the snags.

In Part I of this book, we covered the basis for requiring maximum fall time on a jigging presentation; it's the only time a fish can inhale it because he's usually not going to chase after it like other species might. We also mentioned the idea behind "bulking up" a jig for certain applications. Assuming you've got the right jig (as light as you dare) tied to some thin-diameter mono, such as six or four-pound Stren or Trilene XL, all that's keeping you from becoming a top-notch jig fisherman is concentration.

It is reported that the thinking process of men differs from women significantly: Men concentrate on mainly one thing at a time, while women are capable of "juggling" divergent thoughts. This makes women more sensitive, and men more decisive decision-makers. In light of this, walleye anglers need to know what, specifically, to concentrate on while jigfishing.

Our advice is to focus on the line collapsing on the fall. Whenever the jig hits bottom, it will go limp and collapse. This is the best way to know if you're on the lake floor or not. And when a fish hits, the line will *not* go limp on the fall; your rhythm will be interrupted. This is far superior to trying to feel a "tunk" every time your jig drops. (Of course, you don't want to see the line collapse on every drop; that will cause snags.)

You should also forget about trying to differentiate between a snag and a fish when jigfishing. If something solid registers on your line, set the hook immediately. Get it over with. Find out if it's bottom or a fish, and don't fart around. If you are hesitant, the fish will spit the hook.

Now there's an added requirement for successful jigging that doesn't get much ink. By following the line as it slacks off on the fall *with your rod tip,* as well as with your eye, you'll have much more control than if you merely watch your line and make random jigging strokes. Ideally, you want to see about a three or four-inch bow to your line as you drop your rod tip on the fall. Any less won't allow the jig to free-fall, and any more won't give you enough time to register a take.

Most jig fishermen first realize they've got a fish on the line as they raise their rod on the upswing. Suddenly, a fish will just "be there." That's fine if you end up with the fish in the net. But that doesn't always happen, because it's difficult to get all the stretch out of your line on the hook-set.

There is an antidote to this ailment that Mike has perfected. A faint "tick" usually precedes the unanticipated weight of the fish on your line, and if you learn to look for this telltale sign, you will catch many more fish on a jig than you lose. The tick is the result of the line stretching after a fish has attempted to inhale your bait. It doesn't get any better than this, and you should immediately set the hook when you feel it. In very deep water, in cold weather and in windy conditions, it's tough to feel the tick. Then you should use high-visibility line and watch for unusual twitches on the jig's descent.

Mention jig fishing, and invariably the subject of stinger hooks comes up. A stinger is a trailing hook, typically a small treble hook that's designed to be impaled in the aft end of a minnow. We don't recommend stingers for two reasons. First, they almost always destroy the action of the minnow. So many times we'll see someone getting lots of short hits and then tie a stinger on. Almost like a cold front, the fish will seem to shut off. No more bites. The reason is that the minnow's natural movements are retarded by the additional hook. Apparently, the fish's lateral line can pick this up.

And second, stingers are no substitute for making your presentation go with the flow of the water in the first place. Instead of trying to concoct ways of "tricking" walleyes, we ought to be mastering the sound fundamentals of the walleye game. It's a classic example of majoring in minor matters again.

Mike fishes jigs by watching his line collapse and waiting for "ticks."

Besides a correct attitude and proper concentration, there are other fundamentals to be considered:

• The time to fish jigs is when fish are tight—bunched up in a small area or concentrated along a particular contour or depth. Jigging should not be used to work over scattered fish or to find fish. The lone exception is when fish are on the spawn (or just prior to it) in shallow water. A slow, deliberate presentation is called for. But jigging is usually at its best when you've already located fish and you need longevity in your presentation.

• When *casting* jigs, minnows are a distant third behind leeches and crawlers. Minnows won't take the pounding and are easily cast off without your knowing it —a bad mathematical combination. Leeches, if available, are ideal. Half a crawler, double-hooked in the middle, is just as appealing to a walleye as a whole crawler. Plus, it will let you hook more of those that do bite.

• Minnows are perfect for vertical jigging, but inspect them often; half-dead ones should either be tossed to the seagulls or culled for bullhead fishing. A bow-mounted electric is unbeatable for vertical jigging in deep water. You can stay right over a sharp break or on the inside edge of a cup where fish are packed in tight. First, make contact with the bottom. Then yo-yo the jig close to it with short strokes. It works better than any tactic we know of for deep, cold fish. Occasionally, a walleye might make a fatal nip at a jig dancing like this in front of its snout, even though the last thing on its mind is another meal. Pre-spawn fish are a good illustration of this.

• Vertical jigging two rods is difficult and should be done only as a last resort. A better strategy would be to rig up a slip bobber on your secondary rods. Vary your offerings; perhaps a leech could be hooked to the bobber, while you jig a minnow.

• When casting jigs, don't fight the wind. Hit those shore-lines with an oncoming wind first, even if it means motoring an extra distance. A sideways wind can be just as bad as one in your face. It will blow a big bow in your line and tighten your presentation, even on the fall of the jig. This will make it all but impossible for the fish to inhale it, and you won't be very adept at reading the pickups.

If you can't avoid these winds, try this trick: Use sidearm, *back-handed* casts with your rod tip low to the water. This type of cast will net you the greatest distance, while reducing line belly. To pull it off, however, you will need a close-faced reel;

a Zebco 33 may be ideal for beginners, but it also works wonders under these tough conditions.

Vertical jigging requires total concentration and usually results in total frustration.

• There is a little-known secret involving casting jigs: Holding your rod high during the lift-and-drop retrieve. It will do two things for you. First, getting a more vertical lift on the jig will yield maximum fall time. Thus, a fish will have a better chance of sucking it all the way into its mouth; a jig that falls, say, 10 inches, is neutrally-buoyant much longer than one that only falls two inches.

And second, a more vertical jig presentation will catch more walleyes because it's going to be hung up less. The higher your rod tip, the more easily it will be to skip over rocks, logs and tree branches.

For picking fish off small rock piles, one of the slickest techniques is to cast tiny leadheads with very light line from a long rod—nine feet is about right. Naturally, this rod should be as light as possible, because the added length could detract from its overall sensitivity. And it should be fairly stiff at the tip to telegraph what's going on below. It won't be easy to find a rod with both characteristics, but one particular model does: LCI's Excelon GST 902 is a good measuring stick to compare others to. (It's also excellent for casting slip bobbers on a calm day).

• Color can make a difference. However, if someone is catching fish in the boat and you're not, observe carefully the action that's being imparted to the jig. Color selection has been used as a scapegoat from being responsible for presenting the right bait in the best possible manner.

• Trolling jigs can be very effective, particularly along the edge of a weedbed. Dick Grzywinski, a guide on Lake Winnibigoshish in central Minnesota, has perfected the technique to a deadly science. For optimum control, jigging, like bottom bouncing, should be done at a 45 degree angle or less.

What about the action of a jig? Most anglers don't think in these terms when they think about using jigs. But this can be significant. Only the foundation of attitude and concentration ranks higher.

Action is a chief element in jigfishing. You are the key to a jig's action—a jig will do whatever you make it do. You can twitch it, hop it, drag it or just let it sit there. Which is best? To answer that question, we need to establish what works best under most circumstances, and go from there.

The basic retrieve is one done from a 10 o'clock position to an 11 o'clock one. As discussed, if you keep your rod at this angle during the retrieve, you will get maximum fall time and avoid snags. From this position, you can decide what to do with the rod tip, which will impart whatever action you want to give the jig. The key is to experiment. What works one day may be bogus the next.

A good example of this is a situation Gary Roach and Randy Amenrud found themselves in a few years ago. They were doing some winter promotional work on Lake Norman in Tennessee, when the wind suddenly changed. The temperature dropped and it began to rain. There was only one rain suit in the boat, and somehow Roach ended up with it.

The fish shut completely off, and to make matters worse, Randy got the shakes real bad. He couldn't hold his rod still, and his shivering sent little ripples down his line and onto his jig. All of a sudden he began catching fish, one after another.

"What are you doing different?" Roach demanded.

"N-n-nothing I can t-t-tell," Amenrud said.

Then Roach started shaking. Hoping that he was ready to head back to the landing, Amenrud asked, "You cold, too?"

"Heck no," Roach replied, after he unhooked his second fish in a row. "But I'm no dummy."

As unconventional as it may seem, this is a legitimate way to affect a jig's action and get the attention of the fish.

When it comes to jigging action, Gary Roach is no dummy.

There's more mischief you can dapple with. Recently, Mike has been experimenting with another radical approach. In talking with Ray Eng, who oversees the aquariums Babe Winkelman maintains to photograph and experiment with fish, Mike discovered something he's always known, but couldn't quite put a finger on. So many times he would find a walleye latched onto his jig after he netted a fish for someone else in his boat. Or a fish would "be there" when he first started to pull his jig back, after a long cast had settled to the bottom. Did these fish take the jig *while it was lying on the bottom*?

Eng's observations of the tank fish seem to confirm this mysterious phenomenon. Eng found that negative fish would not respond to any kind of action from a jig, including zinging it by swiftly or jiggling it in front of their noses. But if the jig was allowed to lie on the bottom for 30 seconds or so, often a walleye would ease over. As often as not it would tip up, flare its gills, and suck the jig right off the floor of the aquarium.

Since talking with Eng, Mike has been using the technique of "dunking" jigs a lot more often than he ever thought would be necessary. It has its place in a well-chosen arsenal of presentations, particularly for cold, finicky fish.

The best head design for dunking? If you're catching on, there's an obvious choice: a stand-up head. This style will make it easier for the fish to get the hook barb inside its mouth and will result in higher hooking ratios.

Dunking should not be done in conjunction with dragging the jig across the bottom. This kind of presentation will guarantee short hits, for obvious reasons: no fall time whatsoever. Instead, combine dunking with normal lift-and-drop jigging. Space each extended pause to correlate with bottom contours where dormant fish might be sulking.

Besides dunking, Mike has discovered something about fishing jigs that's also unconventional but has merit. Sometimes merely suspending a jig slightly off the bottom—without doing anything to it—will seduce fish when nothing else will. This is precisely what Randy Amenrud and Gary Roach did to win the 1987 Spring Valley tournament on the Illinois River. Accepted walleye theology would dictate that traditional yo-yoing under these conditions should have been the "only way to go." But the real world apparently said otherwise.

So many times Mike has seen Bob come up with a unique jigging action that later proved to be the pattern of the day. Suspending a jig might be unorthodox, but if it works why fight it?

Don't underestimate how a jig's dressing affects its action.

Another way of imparting action to a jig is by adding differ-ent kinds of dressings to the hook shank. If you don't think this is important, ask Bob Propst. Earlier, we established the fact that fish use their highly developed lateral line organ to read the signatures of moving objects. Propst once owned a Fuzz-E-Grub that looked like most of the others, except this one *really* appealed to the fish. It was unreal. Mike witnessed first-hand the anointing this particular jig had. With it Bob could outfish anybody any time anywhere. Apparently, it had just the kind of underwater vibration that appealed to fish, even though it looked identical to the many clones Bob had in his tackle box.

The point? Don't underestimate the dressing you choose for your jigs. Sometimes bare-shanked jigs work best (usually when smaller offerings are called for); sometimes a fast-actioned jig with a Swirl or Twister-type tail is best (typically for warm-water fish that are hot); sometimes bucktail or maribou might outproduce plastic. Just don't get tunnel-visioned about what to adorn your jigs with. Make comparisons with what worked under similar conditions in the past, but continue to experiment if necessary.

"Crappie jigs" actually make the best walleye jigs. Stock up heavily on 1/6-ounce and 1/8-ounce leadheads.

CHAPTER 14
CRANKBAITS IN DEPTH

I f you took a poll to determine what kind of walleye fishing brings the most satisfaction to the most people, chances are that crankbaiting would top the list. Why? There are many reasons, but two particularly stand out. Crankbaits rank high because they are a sentimental favorite. A majority of us probably began walleye fishing by trolling hardware behind the boat in the prop wash. The image of that first Marble Eye thrashing in the net with a Rapala in its mouth is hard to forget.

But just as important, it's *fun* to catch a walleye with a crankbait! You can set the hook with a degree of confidence right away. There's no dilly-dallying around. Either the fish is there or it's not. And, for some reason, walleyes seem to fight harder when they're clamped onto an artificial than when they're fed live bait with a jig or rig.

Of course there are other reasons to fish crankbaits. They're easily trolled along a shoreline or near the edge of a reef. You can work them at a pretty good clip and cover a lot of ground in a short period of time. And a crankbait won't die on you when you can least afford it; unlike live bait, there's no mess or storage problems to fuss over.

In spite of all these advantages, crankbaits probably cost the average walleye fisherman more fish than they catch. How's that? It's quite simple. Due to their mass appeal, crankbaits are overfished and underestimated; they're used when they shouldn't be, and when they should be used, little forethought goes into their selection and presentation. For some reason, crankbaits are viewed as some sort of cure-all that requires little, if any, finesse.

A peculiar trait among walleye fishermen is that very few of them cast crankbaits for walleyes. Almost everyone trolls these baits. On the contrary, Mike, who spends 250 days a year in a boat, trolls crankbaits no more than five days a year. Why? Because crankbaits have a serious limitation: Due to their design, they will only troll at one depth. For example, a Lindy Shadling's maximum depth will always be 17 feet on six-pound line. You can put it back into your tackle box and take it out next month, but nothing will change; it will still go 17 feet. You can try it in a natural lake or a reservoir; it will still go 17 feet.

Problem is, what if some of the fish are in 14 feet and some are in 22 feet? Granted, you can switch back and forth with different-running crankbaits, but that can be cumbersome and time-consuming. For trolling crankbaits with any degree of efficiency, then, you need four factors going your way: 1) The majority of the fish must be stacked at a specific depth; 2) The depth must be fairly constant; 3) The fish must be scattered; and 4) You must know the exact depth each lure you put out will run.

Why scattered fish? We've already established the important rule of fish location dictating tactics and presentation. With trolling cranks, this is doubly important, because you will have more line out than with live bait rigs; this will take longer to turn your boat around to come back for fish concentrated in a small pocket. Again, playing the odds.

Scattered fish, on the other hand, are a double-edged sword that cuts two ways for you: You'll be able to look for possible fish concentrations *as you troll*, and scattered fish tend to be hot fish—fish that are looking for something to eat. It would generally be fruitless to run a fast-moving bait through the fish if their mood, or metabolism, isn't in tune with your lure speed. The timespan of your presentation should always match the mood of the fish; slow for cold fish, faster for hot fish.

Precise depth control is imperative. The best way to know just where all your baits run is to do a little homework ahead of time, so this information is always at your fingertips. You'll have to find out for yourself, because you can't rely on the manufacturer. Why? No one can predict the three variables that affect a crankbait's depth—line diameter, trolling speed, amount of line let out—except you. Here's a simple experiment you can complete in less than a half hour.

Let your lure out behind the boat, over deep water, the distance you're most comfortable with. Keep in mind precisely how far it is. Then head for shallow water and note what depth the bait finally hits bottom. Now you're ready to record these details in a spiral notebook. Do this for all of your favorite crankbaits, from the shallow-diving minnow-imitators to the deep diving models. You might want to take it a step further and experiment with varying line weights; the difference between six-pound test and 10-pound test can be as much as eight feet with some lures.

The ideal place to conduct this test is over a sandy point with a slow taper. If you do it on a steep slope, you'll get inaccurate readings because your depth finder will be recording much shallower water as your bait hits bottom.

There are a number of ways to compute line distance behind the boat. Some anglers, including Gary Parsons, use level-wind reels for all their trolling. This allows them to count the number of passes the line guide makes each time it crosses the spool. Most of the time this will be a fairly uniform number, unless you break off a considerable hunk of line; a completely full spool will give a different reading than one that's only three-fourths full. The average medium-sized reel pays out between five and eight feet of line per pass, but you should double-check this figure.

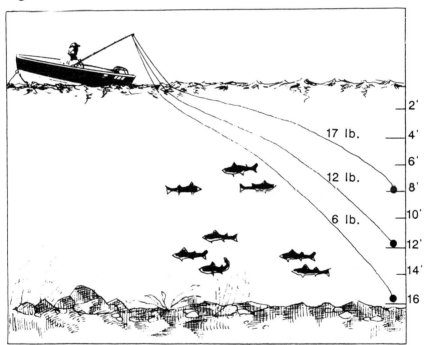

17 lb.

12 lb.

6 lb.

2'
4'
6'
8'
10'
12'
14'
16

Line diameter is a chief factor in determining crankbait depth. It pays to know exactly to what extent.

When using standard, open-face reels Mike counts "rod sweeps." It's as accurate as any method we've heard of. All you have to do is open the bail, put a finger on it, and drop the lure in the water back by the motor. Then sweep your rod tip forward, while lifting your finger temporarily off the bail, to a predetermined point.(You can use a benchmark on the boat, such as an oarlock or a chair. Or, you can stop the rod sweep at an imaginary two o'clock position but, again, you'll have to pre-measure this distance.) Then put your finger back on the bail and follow the slack line back to the starting point. Repeat this until your lure is where you want it.

How far back should you run most lures? For maximum depth, we recommend 75 feet as a ballpark figure. If you let out much more line than that, your crankbait will actually begin to rise; the water pushing against the additional line will add up to more resistance than the lure can dive against.

The ideal situation for trolling crankbaits is a good-sized mud flat, or a reef with a tabletop to it. Many anglers prefer drifting these spots, and that's not a bad idea if the wind speed is sufficient. If it's not, or it suddenly dies on you, get those crankbaits out, but take a few things into account first. They can make a big difference in the outcome.

Topping the list are two unlikely candidates: rod selection and rod position. Should you merely troll four crankbaits over the back of the boat, you'll reduce your chances significantly. Why cover an eight-foot swath, when with longer rods you could easily triple that distance? Two nine or 10-foot rods kept *perpendicular* to the gunwale will cover anywhere from 24 to 32 feet! This is a big advantage when you remember that walleyes are basically lazy feeders and won't move very far to take your bait.

Of all the rods we've tried over the years, our current favorite for long rod crankin' is a Berkley Series One nine-foot steelhead rod (S94-9'MS). It's extremely light, yet the tip is fairly stiff—perfect for trolling crankbaits at moderate speeds or in heavy current.

Spreading your lines out laterally is an odds-maker, but so is staggering your lines vertically. On flats, this isn't a consideration, but with sharp breaks it sure is. The rip rap at the face of a dam, or a long point is easy pickin's with this method. Again, instead of trolling all your baits directly behind the boat at the same depth, run them at depths corresponding to the bottom gradient. If you use long rods it will be a cinch.

On your inside rod, which can reach out and almost touch the bank, run a shallow-runner, like a No. 11 Rapala or Lindy Baitfish. On the rod running underneath the boat, where it's likely to be 10 feet, a Hot 'n Tot or a No. 5 Lindy Shadling, or No. 7 Shad Rap would be an excellent choice. Further out it could be 15 feet. Perhaps a Rattlin' Spoonbill Rebel would just tick bottom. You can continue this scenario with a fourth rod, if necessary.

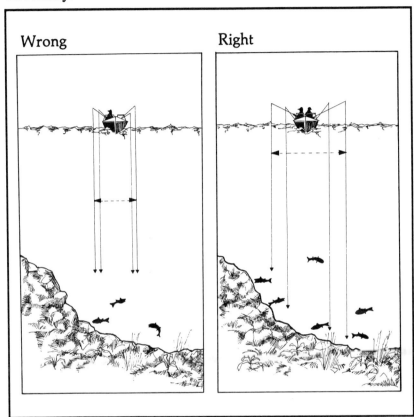

Look at the benefits. Now, instead of fishing one depth zone, you can cover three or four *in one pass* . And besides the bonus of fishing while you're looking for fish, you might be able to catch those walleyes that have darted out from under the boat's wake. If any fish dive into the rocks, the inside rod will cover them. Those taking refuge in deeper water will be taken care of by the outside rod(s). Talk about an odds booster! Credit Bob Propst for perfecting this effective mathematical approach.

TROLLING BOARDS

Some crankbait tactics developed for tackling Great Lakes salmonids also work well on walleyes. Trolling (or planer) boards is one example. On the surface, it might seem like a lot

Gary Parsons with a dandy Winnebago walleye taken with trolling boards.

of rigmarole to go through. And it does require some diligence. But any time walleyes are scattered horizontally *and* vertically, this is the most efficient way to go. If this condition is common on waters near you (Wisconsin's Lake Winnebago, some large southern reservoirs, Lake Erie), we urge you to conquer this system.

A pair of trolling boards should allow you to cover a wide path as well as a multitude of depth zones. Gary Parsons knows this tactic as well as anyone. And he knows what the most essential ingredient is.

"The whole key is attention to details," he maintains. "There is room for error with most other walleye applications, but not this one. A 'trivial' item overlooked could end up taking an hour to unravel."

The basic setup is relatively simple. A board (double or single), attached to 50 to 150 feet of tow cord, is let out on each side of the boat. The board's beveled nose will force it to angle out and behind the boat. Next, you let your crankbait out at a *predetermined* distance and attach your line to a "release." The release, depending upon the type of board you employ, either slides down the tow cord toward the board, or is fastened to the board itself. Finally, your rods are stuffed into rod holders strategically situated inside the boat.

A number of fine points must be observed. First, you must match the depth of your crankbaits to the depth most of the fish are concentrated in. On some days that might be fairly easy to determine. Your sonar could tattle on suspended fish. If they're over fairly deep water (and not too close to the surface) the readings should be reliable. But most of the time trial-and-error will tell you what works best.

Parsons recommends running a variety of plugs at several depths. If one line hooks a fish, he won't change. But if it produces a second fish, he'll switch the rest over and saturate that zone. And should the pattern fizzle, he won't hesitate to raise or lower his lines as he attempts to establish another pattern.

"Trolling boards aren't for the lazy man," he says. "I'm constantly monitoring every rod and analyzing the surrounding conditions. Things are ever-changing, and what works in the morning might not work in the afternoon."

Large trolling boards are ideal for rough seas. A two, three, or even four-foot chop is no obstacle for a pair of double-running boards that are capable of slicing right through the froth.

And lately, some slick collapsible models have been introduced, eliminating the nettlesome problem of storage. (For information on boards and releases, write: Laurvick Release Co., 1411 N. 58th Street, Superior, WI 54880; 715-394-7671.) The main disadvantage of Great Lakes-type boards is that small, light-biting fish might not get hooked; the resistance from a "sliding" release on a tow cord is less than one tied directly to the board.

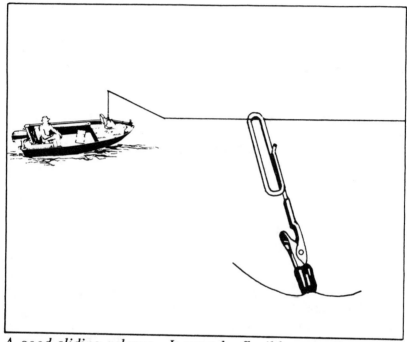

A good sliding release. It must be flexible, yet offer a wide array of tension settings.

For light-biters, consider "releasing" trolling boards, such as the Rover (Troll Sports Inc., 512 Park Place, Stillwater, MN 55082) that attach directly to your rod line. Releasing boards offer several distinct advantages, besides better hooking ratios on soft bites. For one, they're less cumbersome and more easily fished in crowds. For another, they're easier to control; you can adjust distances from the boat by merely retrieving or letting out line from your reel (ideal for irregular points or weedlines).

Releasing boards are also much more responsive to boat direction. A slight curve or small wave will impart immediate action to your lure. And you have some flexibility in how to rig them. For example, Rovers can be rigged so they'll fall off your line after a fish is hooked, or remain on the line as you play it. If you set them up with the latter method, you'll have to manually release your line and be careful to maintain tension on the fish at all times. Parsons actually prefers this because it's not that difficult to do with walleyes, and it eliminates having to double back to retrieve the Rover board.

Standard rods and reels work well with Great Lakes-style boards, although level wind reels might be easier to monitor line distance behind the boat for most anglers. But when fishing releasing-type boards, much stouter rods and heavier monofilament line is required. Choose stiff-tipped actions and go with 12-pound mono on large-capacity level-winds.

Generally, crankbaits and trolling boards are best matched with aggressive, hot fish. But Gary Gehrman from Stillwater, Minnesota, uses releasing boards for cold, negative walleyes. He surprised a lot of folks during at the 1988 Land O' Lakes, Wisconsin (Ciscoe Chain) tournament with his boards 'n cranks. We're convinced that it wasn't dumb luck.

After discussing with Gary Parsons which lake in the Chain might be best suited for his unique board presentation, Gehrman arrived the eve of the tournament. Without the benefit of any pre-fishing, he promptly went out the next morning and took a pair of seven-pound-plus hawgs, the two largest of the two-day event. How'd he do it?

"I knew the fishing pressure on the Chain would put the fish down," he began. "And I knew I would need big fish to place well. So I concentrated my efforts where big fish might be lying away from all the boat traffic."

Virtually every pattern was hard-hit over the weekend—from downed cedars, to rock reefs; from points to deep-water humps. That left only once place untouched: deep, soft-bottomed basins. Gehrman's method produced because he slow-trolled crankbaits right on the bottom.

But there's a lot more to his theory than fish location. He's certain that any fish he takes this way are striking out of a *defensive*, not *offensive*, reaction. And without boards, it's tough to present a bait right on top of the fish. Why? Big walleyes in heavily fished waters, he says, routinely avoid boats trolled directly overhead, and boards are the only way to get a crack at them.

Another important variable to consider is lure action, which is primarily a function of boat speed. Parsons usually runs his boat in a fairly straight course when he's searching for fish.

That way he'll cover more water and eliminate nonproductive areas quickly. But after he's zeroed in on a school of walleyes, he'll change over to controlled S-curve patterns.

As he does this, he's very careful to note exactly what the boat was doing when a fish struck a particular line. Was it while the board was speeding up or slowing down? Specifically where on the turn did the hit occur? Answers to these questions are the best clues to determining lure action. Again, it's mainly a matter of details.

Occasionally, you might find scattered walleyes at depths greater than your crankbaits will run. Then what? Boards may still be the answer, but you'll have to add some weight. There are two routes to go. One is with keel sinkers. With a bead chain they're less likely to twist your line than Rubbercor sinkers. Keel sinkers might take longer to rig up, but when properly outfitted, you'll save time in the long run.

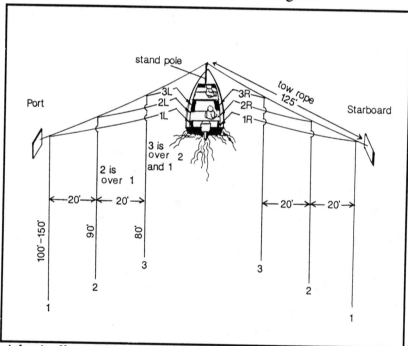

A basically trouble-free Great Lakes trolling board system. To avoid line tangles, study this diagram carefully, or take this book with you.

The biggest complaint with keel sinkers is the time it takes to change weights. Suppose you've got four lines out with four sizes of keel sinkers—a one-ounce, a 1 1/4-ouncer, a 1 1/2-ouncer and a two-ouncer—and the 1 1/2 ounce system proves to be the best depth. How do you quickly switch everything over? Try this leader set up: To the end of your line tie a plain snap, and rig up a six-foot leader (if you're using long rods) with the crankbait on one end and another snap on the other. This arrangement will alleviate all knot-tying and re-tying, and make the transfer of varying lead weights (with bead chains) a snap—literally!

Another option for adding depth to crankbaits—whether they're fished with boards or not—is with leadcore line. Leadcore has been around for decades but, again, Bob Propst is the first walleye professional to really make it work. Bob learned that a virtually snagless deep-water presentation could be created by tying leadcore to a long monofilament leader (20 feet or more) with a nail knot.

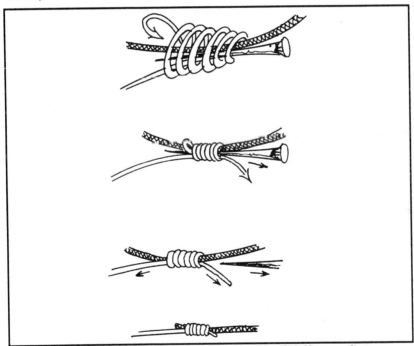

The nail knot is ideal for joining two lines of different diameters; memorize or clip and save.

Bob's favorite lure for leadcore trolling is the Thin Fin. It has three virtues most crankbaits don't have: durability (the lip is a continuation of the body), shallow-running (necessary for

Thin Fins are a good bait for both casting the shallows and running behind leadcore line in deep water.

working behind weighted line) and a slow "walleye wobble."
Now if you're going after suspended fish with trolling boards
(don't use leadcore with releasing-type boards; it's too thick for
their tripping mechanism) Thin Fins aren't necessary. Most any
walleye crankbait will work. But if you'll be doing any bottom-
pounding, Thin Fins are in, and plastic-lipped models are out.

Leadcore is more versatile than you might think. Several
hundred yards can be spooled onto a large-capacity, level-wind
reel (such as a Penn 210). This outfit also doubles nicely for
trout and salmon fishing. Another option is to rig up 30-foot-to-
30-yard sections that can be nail-knotted to the main line on both
ends. This approach is best for smaller-capacity reels. After an
initial orientation period, you will know just how much leadcore
is needed for covering the waters you like to fish. And don't
forget to keep this technical data in your spiral notebook, along
with the other crankbait information.

CASTING

So much for deep-water cranking. Although casting
crankbaits for walleyes usually takes a back seat to pitching jigs,
there are several situations that definitely call for artificials. A
lesson I learned from Mike on my first early-season tournament
on Nebraska's Lake McConaughy, is a good case in point.

After talking to Bob Palser, a veteran guide on the lake,
Mike felt that an isolated section of shoreline might be good for a
stringer of smaller males. We proceeded to cast minnow-imitators against the bank and gleaned several fish. To me, the four-
mile stretch looked pretty much the same: a mixed bag of boulders, fist-sized rocks and scattered pebbles. But Mike carefully
noted precisely where each fish came from.

"It's time to get out the jigs," he said, as he hastily reeled in
a Thin Fin.

"But we didn't do so bad with the crankbaits," I protested.

"True," he said. "But I have a feeling we might have picked
off most of the hot fish. They did their job by helping us pinpoint the best spots. Now we'll go back to each area we took a
fish from and work it over more slowly with jigs."

The strategy paid off. We tripled our catch with the jigs
because a majority of the fish were quite sluggish, requiring
longevity to our presentation. So casting crankbaits in unfamiliar water is an excellent way to zero in on micro structure—
individual rocks or drop-offs that tend to hold the most fish.

To eliminate unproductive water with crankbaits, be sure to memorize each pocket every fish came from, before you leave the area. Look for windy shorelines so you can make long casts and fish the fish before you spook them. And remember that closed-face reel; it will outperform baitcasting models when light line and light lures are used. Again, back-handed casts for quartering winds are better than overhand or ordinary sidearm casts.

Hot fish are best fished by casting cranks, only don't make the mistake of making haphazard casts. Almost always, shallow-water fish will be positioned tight to specific structure. If you miss it by a foot or two, even aggressive walleyes—especially those over two pounds—won't move that far to take your offering. So not only long, but *accurate* casts, are therefore necessary. And when you hook a fish, be sure to fight it out of the pocket immediately, and follow up with another cast to the exact spot.

Common sense dictates that you choose a crankbait to match the contours of the structure you're fishing. A Lindy Baitfish, Thin Fin, or No. 9 Rapala are excellent choices for slow-tapering shorelines. Go with a Shadling or Shad Rap for areas that have a lip with a drop-off. All the fish will be just below the lip, so cast parallel to the shore with plenty of pauses along the retrieve. This is essential.

One of the most common errors we see in all of our fishing travels is poor execution with crankbait casting. For some reason, most anglers think that the bait has enough action of its own, and all they have to do is cover as much ground as possible with it. Nothing could be further from the truth. For optimum performance, your crankbait should look like a minnow that's either strayed slightly from the safety of a school, or is frightened and injured. We suggest you imitate both characteristics. Why? Because that's the kind of signature most likely to initiate a strike response from a moody walleye. He's used to it. It's realistic.

What's not realistic, however, is a minnow buzzing along at a uniform clip for 50 or 60 feet at a time. On the contrary, when we observe baitfish acting out their part in Nature, we see mostly one kind of action: stop-and-go. Two-foot stints are most common. Minnows are fidgety. They're constantly darting from one bottom obstruction to the next. And even when

Mike took this monster 11-pound walleye with a stop-and-go retrieve in 3 feet of water. The fish was released after we took its picture.

they're in open water, they like to put on the skids suddenly; their main defense is their eyes, and they can see best while they're at rest.

It follows that the most effective crankbait presentation is going to be along these lines. A stop-and-go retrieve—peppered with plenty of twitches—will outproduce any other. Remember, nothing in a fish's world tears off like a scared rabbit. Everything darts quickly, then settles down shortly. When you've got fish pinpointed in shallow water, your retrieve should do likewise.

Pauses on a retrieve will also give the fish more time to run down your crankbait, but you can make it even easier on the fish. *Be sure to drop your rod tip* to add some slack line to the bait. Just a couple of inches will do. This added bonus of neutral buoyancy will help a cold fish get the lure sufficiently into its mouth, hopefully on the first attempt.

NEUTRAL-BUOYANCY

Mike discovered the virtues of neutral-buoyancy with crankbaits quite by accident, long before he began fishing for a living. This occurred on Big Stone Lake, on the Minnesota/South Dakota border. On a cool, bright summer day, following a week of hot weather, the fish had suddenly turned off. For days he had been catching limits of nice walleyes along a well-established weedbed by trolling crankbaits. But not now.

Of course, this was a classic cold front, but Mike hadn't realized it yet. He decided to forget the walleyes and go deeper for bass, so he tied on a sinking Rapala. On his first cast, however, he turned up a nasty bird's nest on his reel. After painstakingly unthreading the mess, he found himself fighting a heavy fish that smacked his lure after a couple of cranks on his reel. But it wasn't a bass. It was a walleye!

So that's it, Mike thought. *I'll just fish deeper.* It took about an hour to cover the mile-long weedbed, and it didn't produce another fish. That is, not until he backlashed his reel again. The same thing happened all over again: After Mike unravelled the bird's nest, a fish hit before his lure travelled two feet.

The key? Cold front fish simply need more time before they'll strike a moving bait. Mike soon discovered that one of the best presentations for these fish is a neutrally-buoyant crankbait that can be hovered like the Goodyear blimp in the strike zone; when he switched to floaters with just enough split-shot to weight them down, but not sink them, his "luck" changed dramatically.

Earlier, we covered the bases on how to maintain precise depth control for scattered fish over uniform structure. But what about fish tight to the bottom along the edge of a drop-off, or tucked back in cups? Cold fronts and fishing pressure will do this, making standard crankbait trolling impossible. There's only one way to tackle this problem—with a bottom bouncer. Because the bottom bouncer has no conscience, it will drop to whatever depth it's in (provided you've let enough line out). You can be tricky and troll a shallow-diving crankbait about six feet behind the bottom bouncer and cover uneven contours. Lindy Baitfish, Thin Fins and No. 9 Rapalas are ideal for this operation.

It pays dividends to fish neutrally-buoyant crankbaits, and not just for cold front walleyes. Trouble is, most models either float or sink, and there aren't many "in-betweeners" available on tackle shelves. My all-time favorite is Rebel's Rattlin' Spoonbill. I also like doctored baits: drilled and filled floating Rapalas, Thin Fins, etc. Mike still prefers to crimp on several small split-shot, inches ahead of his crankbaits. Recall that this tips the head of the bait forward and is almost snagless—a perfect presentation for tournament conditions.

If you wish to doctor your own baits, consider the following tips. Remember, your goal is to come up with a bait that rises very s-l-o-w-l-y at the pause of a retrieve.

• The general procedure is quite simple. First determine the plug's center of gravity by balancing it on top of a knife. Second, get a good estimate of how much weight will be necessary for the particular make and model by affixing double-sided tape *on both sides* of the body. (This is necessary for counterbalancing weights that will be added to the plug.) Keep adding weight, one on each side, until you arrive at the magic figure; a combination of BBs or No. 5 split-shot will work for most crankbaits.

Finally, drill the appropriate amount of holes, making sure that your drill bit matches the outside diameter of each corresponding weight. Carefully crimp each one securely with a pliers. We've found that six-minute epoxy works best for sealing and waterproofing crankbaits.

• Foam-filled baits, such as the Lindy Shadling, can be drilled and filled, but be prepared to use differing weights for each plug; air pockets are formed during production, and plugs of this type of construction may vary more than those made of balsa or plastic.

• Plastic floaters can be tinkered with by simply injecting some water with a hypodermic needle. All you do is make a small hole by first heating a sewing needle with a match. After filling the bait, seal the hole with epoxy. Once you figure out the correct amount of water, keep a record of it.

It's easy to see how a crankbait can be cast and retrieved with a neutrally-buoyant presentation, but how can trolled plugs be given the same treatment? After all, you can't stop your rods by stopping the boat on a dime ... or can you? Well, by making a lot of turns, as opposed to charting a straight course, you can accomplish the same objective. Try small ones and wider ones. You'll not only find out what trolling speed seems to be most effective, but the inside lines will slack off, thus giving the fish some "play." Here's betting that inside lines will produce the most hits, for obvious reasons.

A frequently asked question involving crankbaits is "What's the best way to tie them up?" Some advocate hard-to-tie, impossible-to-memorize loop knots. Others recommend snap swivels. Both answers are half-truths.

For trolling—especially at night or with boards—light, *rounded* snaps get the nod. Snaps are trouble-free and under these conditions there are enough things to tend to. Still, there are a couple of obstacles to steer clear of when going with snaps.

First of all, a ball bearing swivel (or better yet, a bead chain) tied three to five feet above the snap will eliminate virtually all line twist. We do not recommend a combination snap swivel for most crankbaits, particularly those with a delicate, wide wobble (most thin, minnow-imitators); you can probably get away with a snap swivel when using long-lipped, deep-diving cranks, however. Second, avoid those snaps with a tapered head; they will restrict the side-to-side play of the bait.

When casting cranks, a Bowline knot is an ideal terminal connection. It has three distinct advantages: Better "touch," decent strength and simplicity (to tie *and* remember). On top of all this, the loop it creates allows the bait to swing freely, giving a wider latitude of action to the lure. This knot, like the nail knot, is a "must" for all serious crankbait fishermen. You never know when your last snap might disappear.

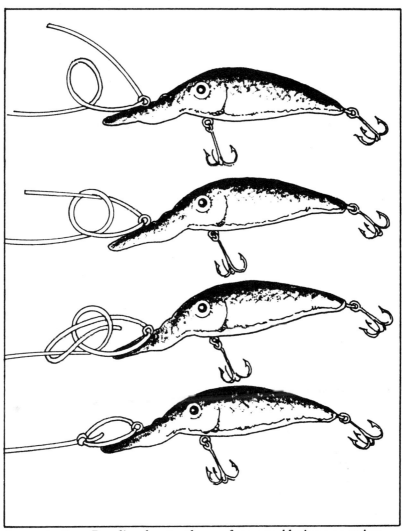

Learn to tie a Bowline knot—the perfect crankbait connection.

Do you know the secret to hooking walleyes with crankbaits? Oh, how many times we've heard the exclamation, "Can't believe the fish missed it!" Fact is, fish don't get hooked that well with crankbaits, in spite of all the treble hooks. Reason? Most anglers don't know how to "feed" crankbaits to walleyes.

Bob Propst rummages through his tackle box for just the right crankbait. There's more to crankbait selection than action or depth.

Suppose you're trolling or casting your favorite bait near a fishy point. You can feel the lure vibrating, and everything is in order. As you turn around to ask Joe how deep the depth finder is reading, something funny happens. But you don't know what.

Instinctively, you set the hook. Nothing there. This happens several times before Joe finally catches a fat four-pounder. What gives? Well, you missed several "hits" and Joe lucked out. However, if you would have dropped your rod tip, rather than jerk it forward immediately, you might have landed a fish or three before Joe got his.

This is quite common with crankbaits. The fish sucks enough water surrounding the bait to temporarily interrupt its action. Momentarily the lure quits vibrating, missing a couple of beats. That feels "different." Next time this happens to you, fight off the urge to set the hook right away. Instead, drop the rod, give the fish a little slack, and then drive it home.

CHAPTER 15
DOWNRIGGING WALLEYES

I f there was a particular lure that, under certain circumstances, absolutely murdered walleyes, would you be interested in it? What about a pattern that produced nice fish when all the traditional ones failed—would you like to know about it?

Now that I have your attention, here's your answer: downrigging. I had to approach the subject from the back door, because if I said up front that all walleye fishermen should add a pair of downriggers to their ever-growing equipment list, I'd probably raise more eyebrows than interest. But it's true. At times, downriggers will murder walleyes and work when traditional methods fail.

A case in point is a trip I made a couple of summers ago when I fished Lake of the Woods, a huge Canadian shield body of water, with well-known fishing educator Tom Zenanko. Now Zenanko had made this trip before, and he virtually guaranteed a cooler full of eaters with several "photo" fish in the eight to 10-pound range tossed in for good measure. He turned out to be a prophet.

Our hosts, Steve Ballard of Ballard's Resort and Mike Truman of Borderview Lodge in Baudette, Minnesota, had a 27-foot fiberglass Sportcraft fully decked out with Cannon downriggers. Their dexterous boat, depth and rod control produced an igloo cooler so full we couldn't close the lid. And, just as Zenanko prophesied, the two largest fish topped out close to 10 pounds. It was a classic example of wisely matching tactics to meet conditions at hand. And Ballard summed it up well when he confided that normal Lindy rigging would have netted a fraction of the fish we caught that day.

Now the acid test for deciding whether to go to the "trouble" of rigging up this system—or any system, for that matter—is efficiency. Again, playing the odds. If it outproduces other tactics, why not go with the flow? But how can a complicated presentation like a downrigger be more efficient for a fish like a walleye?

Good question. Obviously, you must know your equipment. Just as important, you must be able to recognize those unique set of circumstances that make downrigging a percentage shot. This tactic is hardly a universal approach. Below is some straight talk on the when's, where's and how's, including the basics and the fine points.

For starters, let's not make downrigger fishing more complicated than it really is. The overall operation is actually quite simple. I'm about as handy as a monkey with a wrench, and I don't have any trouble with downriggers. Ditto for my wife, Corie. Downriggers are effective because they're one of the best methods for fishing precise depths without any guess-work.

The Wil-Jer stacker is the author's favorite downrigger release.

The system utilizes a lead weight, commonly referred to as a "cannonball," that's attached to a large-capacity reel by a steel cable. The "reel" feeds cable to the cannonball off a boom, or arm, which keeps everything away from the boat (especially your motor). Before you lower the weight to a desired depth, however, you let your lure out behind the boat and attach it to the weight with a "release." This is a similar operation to trolling boards, except everything is underwater. When a fish hits your lure, the release trips and allows you to play the fish free and unencumbered.

A basic tenet of downrigger fishing is matching the tension of your release to the weight, or impact, of the fish's strike. This is easy for trout and salmon, because they really smack a bait. You can get away with mistakes on these fish, but not on lighter-biting walleyes. Therefore, your releases must not only be sensitive, but accurately set. If they're too loose, the fish will trip the mechanism without getting hooked; if the releases are too tight, you could conceivably end up dragging a small fish around for hours without knowing it.

The answer? Be wise and choose a well-designed release. We've tried all kinds, and we highly recommend Black's release and the Wil-Jer (stacker type). Both models meet the three criteria every walleye release must have: A wide array of tension settings; the ability to get a tight rod arc above, without going to a heavy setting on the release below; and no line-pinching. All three are crucial in walleye fishing, where 10 to 12-pound mono is standard gear, and even large fish barely trip a typical salmon/trout release.

Also, you must learn by "feel" what a "proper" setting is. Don't worry. A single day of on-the-water experimenting will educate your fingertips well.

Like most trolling applications, level-wind and baitcasting reels offer distinct advantages over open-faced reels for down-rigger fishing. You can get by, if finances are tight, but if you're looking for an excuse to purchase some new equipment, look no further: Level-winds are simpler to operate, have smoother drags and, as previously discussed, are easiest to gauge the amount of line let out behind the boat. This last factor can be important for two reasons.

First, the "lead," or distance behind the cannonball, can be the difference between filling out and an empty cooler; in clear or relatively shallow water, you need longer leads (up to 50 feet, although 15 to 25 feet is usually sufficient). However, longer leads are always more difficult to fish with, especially when structure is involved.

And second, a most effective presentation is to run all of your lures in a tight grouping, the same distance behind the boat. This gives the illusion of a school of baitfish, and open-water fish accustomed to preying on large schools of shad or alewives are more vulnerable to this setup. Of course, this becomes an impossible task if you aren't capable of determining lure distance, *in every instance*, behind the boat. Again, for most anglers, counting line passes on level-wind reels is the answer.

Rod selection? Long rods again get the nod. You'll get more control out of an eight or nine-footer than with a standard six-foot model, especially when a large fish makes last-minute runs underneath the boat. A longer rod will also increase hooking

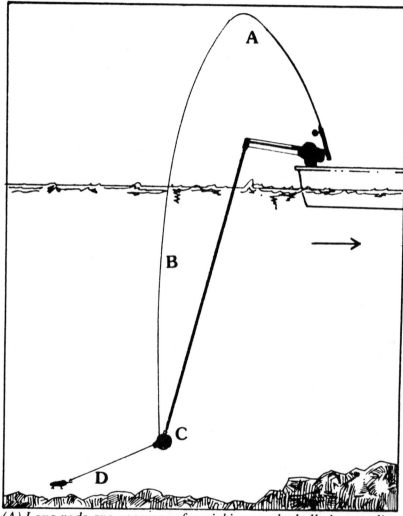

(A) Long rods are necessary for picking up the belly in your line (B) after a fish hits; the cannonball (C) should be lowered within several feet of the bottom so your crankbait (D) can flirt with bottom contours in the strike zone.

ratios by snapping up the belly of the line during that critical period when a fish trips your release. Choosing a rod blank is mainly a matter of personal preference. Ideally, it should be lightweight for maximum sport, with a sensitive tip and strong butt section.

Rigging a boat with downriggers can take a couple of minutes (C-clamping a pair of portables to the gunwales) or a day (permanently mounting electric models). The only precaution is that you should mount the units to the rear of the boat, but away from the motor. This way, tight turns won't tangle the cables and lines, or interfere with playing a fish and navigating the boat.

What areas are best suited for downrigging? We already know that fish location dictates tactics and presentation. So any time you've got hot walleyes at prescribed depths, downrigging could work for you. However, in many instances boards might be a better choice because they cover a wider swath. But if most fish are positioned squarely along a particular drop-off, and it's a uniform bottom, you've got an ideal situation for downriggers. Nighttime is the other classic example, as walleyes suspend well off the bottom, but near structure.

Does this rule out structure fish? Undulating bottom contours do make downrigger fishing "interesting." All it takes is one cannonball wrenched in a rocky crevice, and you'll quickly learn to avoid hangups at any cost. So reefs are out? Not at all. On the contrary, at a certain time of the year this can be the hottest method to take reef walleyes. But it has to be done properly for it to be effective. There are four rules that must be observed.

The first one is timing. The metabolic rate of the fish must be in high gear. Frankly, most of the time walleyes won't respond to this kind of presentation, and no amount of finessing is going to help. The main ingredient, then, is water temperature—the warmer, the better. The so-called dog days of summer are really ripe for rippin' huge walleyes with downriggers. This eliminates much of the fishing season for Upper Midwest anglers, but this limitation pales against those memorable days when every other tactic is fruitless.

Speed is the second rule of the game. Until downriggers came along, only northern pike and bass fishermen could get in on the phenomenon of "speed trolling." Walleyes typically hold too tight to structure at this time of year, and feed availability is at a seasonal high. You have to get their attention, and the best

way is to zip the right kind of lure past them three, four, maybe five miles an hour. It will make the most seductive live bait seem like a bare hook presentation!

What kind of lure are we talking about? The third rule is to stick with crankbaits. By setting your cannonballs safely above the bottom, you can let a crankbait dive down and work the drop-off—where most of the overstuffed fish will be.

And fourth, you must follow the very edge of the reef. (Trolling weedbeds also works, but the fish must be close to the weedline, not within it.) Add these factors together, and you have all the necessary ingredients. It's not much different from a good recipe: If the directions aren't followed, don't expect many dinner guests!

Here are the fine points to the system.

• There is a tricky combination of cannonball depth and crankbait depth that works best. Use this guideline: Run your cannonballs three to five feet off the bottom and your crankbaits within two feet of it. (For 20-foot depths, the cannonballs would be set at 17 feet; use "middle-running" crankbaits that dive two or three feet on a short line.)

• The most effective crankbaits have been these mid-range models: Rebel Fastrac Shads, Lindy Shadlings and Shad Raps. Hottest color combinations are fluorescent orange/gold and fluorescent blue/white. This is one time that blushing fluorescents outdo crankbaits in natural color patterns.

• Speed isn't that critical because these lures will tolerate faster clips. Start at 2 1/2 mph and work your way up the ladder. Don't be surprised if 4 1/2 mph speeds surpass slower ones.

• To stay on the cutting edge of the reef, use marker buoys. It may take over a dozen to establish a trolling pattern on some structure. Take your time and run the reef carefully, making sure to place each marker at the same depth along the drop-off.

• Electric downriggers are better suited than manuals for speed trolling crankbaits. If your boat should accidentally drift off course up on the reef, a flip of a switch will raise your cannonballs out of danger. Penn Fathomaster 820s are an excellent choice.

• Night fishing calls for a different approach. Troll minnow-imitators much more slowly near (or on top of) reefs, not necessarily on the very edge. And long leads with wide S-curves are superior to shorter ones with zig-zags. Most fish are in a pseudo-suspending mode at this time.

Yes Virginia, there is a time for downriggin' walleyes, and the dog days are it!

• If a plug snags bottom, quickly give it line but keep trolling. Most of the time the lure will pop back up, allowing you to reel it back in (while your rod tip is held high).

• Look for untapped frontiers that downriggers might help crack. Besides speed trolling reefs in dead summer, any fishery with a suspended forage base could be ripe—Canadian shield lakes with ciscoes; gizzard shad in Southern reservoirs; large insect hatches in natural lakes; and alewives or herring in the Great Lakes.

These are the basics and enough refinements to point you in the right direction... which, of course, is down!

CHAPTER 16
SLIP BOBBER SECRETS

R eefin' walleyes has been in vogue since the 1960s, when sonar equipment first showed us that we could catch fish away from shoreline structure. But it wasn't until the late 1970s that anglers had a tool for combing every square inch of a reef and making life difficult for resident fish. That tool is the slip bobber. It is responsible for turning average fishermen into deadly predators, according to Jerry Anderson.

"Look at the night ban and the size limit [only one fish over 20 inches is allowed] on Mille Lacs," Jerry said. "The slip bobber is the reason. Folks no longer need to master expert boat control, nor do they have to deal with all the snags in the rocks. Nowadays, it's anchors away, and bobber fishing does it all for you."

If that sounds simple, it is—at least for Anderson. He's the premier expert on reef walleyes and slip bobber fishing. Nobody has paid their dues and reaped the harvest Anderson has. But there's way more to "corking" walleyes than merely anchoring upwind and tossing a bobber with live bait out. Before we look at Anderson's rules to the game, let's take a moment to analyze the weaknesses and strengths of the system.

Slip bobbers are not a wise choice for scattered fish. Forget about flats, tapering points and long, uniform drop-offs. The approach is way too time consuming to hit these areas with any mathematical edge.

Also, depths greater than 25 feet are usually a poor choice for bobbers for two reasons. One, it takes too long for the bait to settle on the bottom. And two, deep fish on uniform bottoms move a lot; you should use your electronics to stay with them, which definitely rules out anchoring and corkin'.

But whenever you've got fish cornered—on reefs, pockets within a weedline, a group of boulders—in tight spaces, this tactic could top the others. There's yet another situation that calls for bobbers. Many times fish will fall to a bait suspended below a bobber when they'll ignore every other presentation. Why? The so-called "bobber bite" is legitimate and there is a rational explanation for it.

For turned-off fish, a long-lasting presentation is often required. If fish are reluctant to follow your offering any distance, the longer you "tease" them with a bait *where they can*

Jerry Anderson is the undisputed king of slip bobber fishing.

eat it, the better your chances are of scoring. When you compare every other walleye tactic, nothing comes close to matching the slip bobber in this respect. So, before you pull up and head for the dock, try slip bobbers.

On an unfamiliar lake, Anderson prefers to look for reefs first. He targets multi-structure areas—those with humps, rock piles, bars, islands and weeds—adjacent to deep water. Then he breaks each area down on a micro scale, looking for structure on structure. This is the key.

"When someone tells me they've found a good reef," Anderson says, "I immediately ask them how many rocks are on it. Usually they can't answer my question, and that tells me they've only done half their homework."

Rocks are important to Anderson because he knows that they will always harbor the biggest fish on a reef. Boulders are hard to beat as an ambush site, and certain areas of a reef will cough up fish in the five to 10-pound range, while others are only good for eaters. Furthermore, bigger reefs usually mean a more diversified menu for the fish; more options always lead to bigger walleyes. Instead of mainly young-of-the-year perch, there could also be crayfish, shiners and occasional schools of tullibees or shad.

Translation? Break a reef down. Don't be satisfied with merely knowing where the steep drop-offs and the gradual ones are. Find the stair-steps, the largest boulders, weeds (if present), spirals and points of the reef. The perfect time to get to know a reef is when the wind isn't blowing. In calm water you might be able to see more clearly what the size and shape of the rocks are but, more importantly, when the wind blows you shouldn't be wasting your time learning the structure—you should be fishing it!

"Wind is like a dinner bell," Anderson insists. "Walleyes are great opportunists, and they don't have to eat every day like we do. But when the wind blows, they'll turn on. It's unbelievable how shallow big walleyes will feed during the day in a good chop. If you look into the waves hard enough, you can actually see them sometimes."

Examining a reef with a microscopic eye is only half of Anderson's two-part formula for graduating from sandlots to the big leagues. Once structure on structure is accurately charted, you must understand *fish movement alleys* on a reef. Walleyes do not swim up the contours indiscriminately, nor do they stop at random depths as they move up a reef or bar. Your answer to these "alleys" boils down to two words: wind direction.

"The upwind side of a reef is always going to harbor the most active fish," Anderson says. "If the right combination of cover and depth is present, that's where you should fish. There could be 100 boats on a given reef, but only one or two spots will be worth a nickel."

Where's the jackpot?

"The arm, or point, of the reef that's running headlong into the wind is unbeatable. Of course, whenever the wind shifts, your hotspot will vary accordingly."

Besides wind direction, the surrounding depth and time of the year could be a major clue as to which side of the reef will attract the most (and largest) fish. In the spring, or early summer, walleyes prefer the shallower, warmer side of a reef; later on, they'll use the deeper, cooler side.

To illustrate both points, Anderson tells of a tournament he won on Minnesota's Mille Lacs Lake, using this principle of fish movement to his advantage (and to the disadvantage of 50 other boats). It was no secret as to which reef he was going to fish. Further, it was common knowledge that one particular underwater point on the reef usually gave up the biggest fish. That's where most of the competition was hovered over.

However, once Anderson cruised the area, he noticed that most of the baitfish showed up in the eight-foot-range on his flasher. He also detected a much smaller arm spiraling off the point out into deep water. Instead of joining the crowd, he anchored off the smaller point and suspended leeches below slip bobbers. By the end of the day, he boated 50 fish, while the other boats combined for about 15.

"We had the spiral to ourselves," Anderson recalled. "We whacked the fish off as they poked their heads up over the eight-foot stair-step. We waited them out, and we were like a deer hunter with the perfect stand location."

From years of experience, Anderson knew that this distinctive structure-on-structure spot would produce. By intercepting the fish as they moved up the water column, without spooking them, he played the odds with a perfect presentation. That's what makes slip bobbers so deadly. In Chapter 11, we flushed out the details on how to get into position to make this all happen. Anchoring is the crucial element. Using the wind, together with a long rod, will also help. But there are many other fine points that make the system even more deadly.

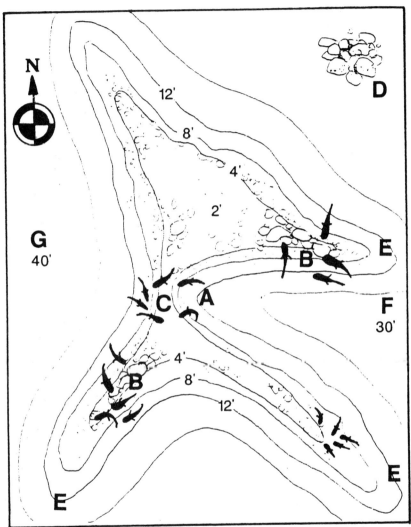

To fish a reef to the fullest extent, you need to break it down on a microscale. Consider the following pointers: Points E will produce fish with southerly winds, but Area B is prime because of the large boulders. Also, C is a natural funnel worth investigating, and D could always house a big fish or two (but not many smaller ones). Finally, the side of the reef closest to F will be more productive than G during spring and early summer; side G will be best during summer and fall.

One of the most important details that's probably beyond the conscious level of most anglers is the rate, or speed, of the float. Over the years, Anderson has learned that by reducing the bobber's rate of travel by 25 percent from what the wave action is, he'll catch twice as many fish. There are several ways to slow the float down. One is to use smaller sizes that catch less water, but they are harder to control and more difficult to cast.

Another way is to use larger bobbers and weight them down so they're barely visible on the surface. Split-shots and /or a jig work fine. The proper amount depends on the kind of float you use. For example, a pencil-shaped foam float should be matched to a single No. 5 split-shot and a 1/32-ounce jig; a fatter Carlisle float might take three split-shots and an eighth-ounce jig, or two split-shots and a quarter-ouncer. A few models even have a lead ring at the base of the neck for adding weight. Jerry Anderson prefers balsa or lead-weighted styrofoam floats because they cast better and are a larger target to keep an eye on in choppy waters.

The above pointers—working concentrations of fish, dissecting the reef, determining walleye movement alleys, reducing the bobber's sweep in the waves—are the foundations of the slip bobber system. Below are a few finishing touches.

• Using a jig instead of a bare hook will do many things for you. Since 1980, Anderson has been experimenting with small leadheads. He likes the control he gets from the added weight *at the bottom of the rig*, as well as the many color options a jig provides.

• The most logical way to eliminate water with slip bobbers is by fishing the deep water first, and working your way up the drop-off. The best way to do this is to cast directly behind the boat and let the float dance its way toward the reef. Casting off to the side is also an option, but most of the action is still going to be behind the boat, since that's where all the bobbers are going to end up. Hint: Have the stern area of your craft clear of clutter!

• Of all baits, leeches are a clear winner for slip bobber fishing. Even on calm days they dance seductively, but be sure to check them often to make sure they're holding up their end of the bargain. (However, don't make the mistake of using half-dead "jumbos" that are at the end of their life cycle; they fade fast in warm water.) A healthy leech's durability is unmatched, allowing long casts while avoiding the hassle of inadvertently tossing the bait off and fishing "naked."

• Just as all reefs are not created equal, not all areas of a reef are created equal. Some sections attract both numbers and good sizes of fish, while others hold relatively few fish. Should we try to distinguish the two? Does a fat dog sleep?

The premier place to look for, according to Anderson, is an *arm* of the main reef that has several large boulders straddling it. Another detail to hunt for is a cut, or stair-step, on the reef; fish definitely stage as they cruise up a reef, and a sudden rise of an otherwise flat area will always stack fish. Sometimes, the difference might only be a foot or two, but it is a very important feature. A third subtlety is where smaller rocks suddenly give way to larger and larger ones.

• There are no magic depths of a reef... or are there? Everything is variable, but here are a few generalities worth pondering: A reef topping out at four feet, with a majority of water lying in 10 to 13 feet is ideal; deep water (30 to 40 feet) adjacent to the reef is also ideal; a grouping of large boulders, in nearby 20-foot water, will not attract many fish, but they will be big; and the eight- to 12-foot stair-step is always a consistent producer.

• Once a fish is caught, pay attention! Throw successive casts in exactly the same spot, making sure to duplicate the depth that's been set on the original rod. Likewise, never cast twice to the same spot until the fish are located.

• Never toss out a bait and let it just sit there. Always work it. Try jiggling, twitching, sliding or even jerking it. The flatter the day, the more necessary this becomes.

• Slip bobbers are great for negative fish, but they might also be the most effective tactic for extremely hot fish. Gary Parsons has discovered that he can occasionally create a "frenzy" by continually dumping bobbers in a pocket that has just produced a fish. One day he and his partner took a fish with a bobber during a tournament on Wisconsin's Lake Winnebago. They decided to toss all four bobbers in the same spot, and all four went down—immediately.

"In states that allow multiple lines, slip bobbers give you the rare bonus of being able to fish while you're netting a fish," Parsons explained. "This makes for a real odds-maker. But you've got to be careful not to blow the school out."

• Parsons rigs his slip bobbers in a unique manner. He uses an egg-shaped slip sinker on the main line, above a three-foot leader of four or six-pound mono. His main line usually consists of 10-pound mono. This way, if the jig (or split-shot

Jeff unhooks a 7-pound walleye that was intercepted by a leech below a bobber at a stair-step on a reef; the fish couldn't refuse this offer. Moments later, another good fish hit from precisely the same spot.

above the hook) should get hung up, he won't lose the bobber. All he'll have to do is break off the lighter line and tie up another short leader. It's the most time-efficient slip bobber rig we've seen, although it sacrifices casting distance with the heavier main line. A nine-foot rod (here we go again) could compensate.

• All too often guys complain about losing too many fish while float fishing. This should not be. Hooking walleyes with this rig takes some getting used to but, once accomplished, it is one of the best in the walleye game (close to 90 percent). There are two important factors that cannot be overlooked: the amount of time you give the fish once the float disappears, and slack retrieval before you set the hook. There is a definite technique to it all.

First, let the fish tell you how long you need to let that bobber stay under water—the first bite usually foretells a pattern. Some days it will be five seconds; others it may be as long as 30 seconds. Ten to 15 is about average. And second, you must retrieve *all* of the slack before you set the hook. Premature hook sets are common, usually costing more fish than "waiting too long." To avoid this, it is important that you actually feel the weight of the fish—not the line merely tightening—before you attempt to move the fish and, thus, set the hook. It's an unusual sensation, but one that will treat you right every time.

Now you don't need reefs to catch walleyes with slip bobbers. There are plenty of situations that are tailor-made for this technique. One of the best is weeds. Earlier, we explained the Jekyll-Hyde nature of walleyes during twilight periods. By first identifying the pockets and openings within a good weedbed during daylight hours, you'll be close to where walleyes are likely to filter through as the sun sets (or rises). Slip bobbers are the best way to fish these "feeding lanes."

Corking walleyes that are stacked under brush and submerged terrestrial vegetation can be deadly, too. As the Texas telemetry study pointed out, walleyes often prefer this kind of cover over reefs and humps. Flooded reservoirs and high spring waters in rivers and natural lakes are classic areas where this bite is likely to be the predominant one. To cash in, it will take some forethought.

The key for wood is the hook. Light-wire Aberdeen hooks are best when combined with fairly heavy line. You won't need light mono below a bobber, as is generally the case for jigging, because the rig is neutrally-buoyant enough. Of course you will get snagged up regularly if your offering is going to penetrate

Another wood walleye bites the dust. This one came from inside *the outer edge.*

the thick stuff. No matter. The fine-diameter hook can be easily bent and pulled free from the wood. This can be done gingerly so as not to spook the fish, and it will save valuable time re-tying hooks.

A long rod (maybe a cane pole?) is perfect for this situation. If you quietly motor in for the kill with your electric, you can actually try "dipping" the various pockets within the wood.

Joe Bucher, a full-time guide from northern Wisconsin, has done some original work with walleyes in wood, and he's noticed that the average angler makes two mistakes when fishing this pattern. One involves shade—often a crucial element for fish location.

"If you pay attention to the shoreline's orientation to the sun," he told me, "you'll find out why certain stretches produce fish in the morning and others in the afternoon. The main reason is that the fish want deep-water access on the shade side of a stump or tree, and if it's not available, they might not use that particular drop-off."

Besides shade, the other important pointer to keep in mind is to fish the shallowest portions of cover before moving on. According to Bucher, these areas routinely hold as many fish as the tip of the structure, but many fishermen have a hard time believing that walleyes live that shallow. We know better, don't we?

Some snags are inevitable, but if you use the proper terminal setup, you can eliminate 90 percent of your hang-ups. Joe Bucher manufactures a Brush Hook that has a unique wire guard. It's perfect for "bushwhacking." If you elect to use a jig while wood fishing—either below a bobber or for casting —try Jack's "brushguard jig" (Jack's Jigs, 2545 South Delaware Ave., Milwaukee, WI 53207).

CHAPTER 17
KEEP CURRENT WITH RIVER WALLEYES

D id you know that there are more than 900,000 rivers in the Lower 48 states, and about half of them harbor fishable populations of walleyes? In spite of the meteoric rise in popularity of the walleye in recent times, rivers are like a fruit tree in season, fully ripe for harvesting. It's baffling because we can usually catch more fish on a typical river, day in and day out, than on most natural lakes and impoundments.

Why is that? Two reasons. First, river walleyes are generally more aggressive than their lake-dwelling counterparts. The current sweeps their food by, and they are conditioned to react quickly or let the morsel go. This makes picky presentations, such as jigging much easier. And second, we can usually coax a few river fish during the thick of a roaring cold front. Not so with lake fish. Put the two together, and you have a whale of a fishery.

Yet, for some reason, a majority of walleye fishermen feel more comfortable on a lake than on a stretch of current. Part of the reason might be a recent trend in the tackle industry. Bigger, lighter boats with more fuel-efficient motors, and innovations like trolling boards and downriggers, have combined to make fishing on open-water expanses relatively easy. This has greatly helped to unlock the expanding fisheries on Lake Erie, reservoirs in the West and Midwest, Southern impoundments and many large Canadian shield lakes.

The real revolution in walleye fishing, however, has been in the field electronics. Before the advent of sonar, nobody fished mid-lake structure, such as humps, reefs, flats and submerged weedbeds. Nowadays, everybody does. Today, a guy can motor for hours by Loran coordinates to an underwater target and be greeted by 100 boats!

But on rivers, most of this paraphernalia is little more than wasted space and extra weight. Thoreau's famous admonition to *simplify, simplify* is the best piece of advice for river fishing. Instead of sensitive electronic equipment for reading what's going on beneath the surface, we need to be sensitive to what's going on at the surface of the river. It's a back-to-basics type of fishing, and your ability to tune into the physical environment— not a CRT screen—is your greatest asset.

Common lake strategy won't net you a lot of river fish, either. River fishing isn't difficult, just different. Let's make the distinctions and get right down to it!

All of the rules we've established in this book still apply to river fishing, such as fish location dictating tactics and presentation. But there's another ingredient that adds a subtle twist to the affair—current. If you've ever wondered why a particular reef or point in a lake produced, while a nearly identical one didn't, try this one on: Fish-attracting structure in rivers must not only have the right composition and the right depths, but they must also have the right amount of current if they're going to hold many walleyes on a given day.

The kicker is that rivers are constantly changing—almost daily. Rarely do they stay at the same depth, with water clarity remaining unchanged, for long. Even during near-monsoon conditions, lake levels rise by the inch. Rivers typically rise and drop by the foot during periods of moderate rainfall. The implications are obvious. You've got to stay on top of the fish and let memories fade away if they don't produce after the first or second pass.

To simplify the business of fish location, there are only two rules to follow for catching river fish. One is to remember that a walleye is basically a lazy fish, similar to an overweight old-timer who doesn't like walking uphill or going against the wind, let alone tackling both at the same time. And that's precisely what a river is to a walleye wherever the current is strongest. At the same time, however, the fish need cover. Add these two factors up, and you'll have fish location down pat most of the time.

Obstructions (wing dams, rocks, logs, pilings) reduce current and also create pockets of deep water in the river bed. They're excellent places to begin your search, and you can read them like a book; the surface will be slack and bubbles often break on the surface, and sometimes the current direction will reverse itself (eddies).

But, as we just said, things change. The back side of a bar could be stockpiled with fish on Monday, and be totally void of fish on Wednesday. To narrow down your search, take a good look at the river's height and rate of flow. A general rule worth memorizing is that when the current is really up, pockets behind (and ahead of) obstructions *near shore* will attract the most fish; when the river is down, such structure *away from shore* and closer to the main channel will hold the most fish.

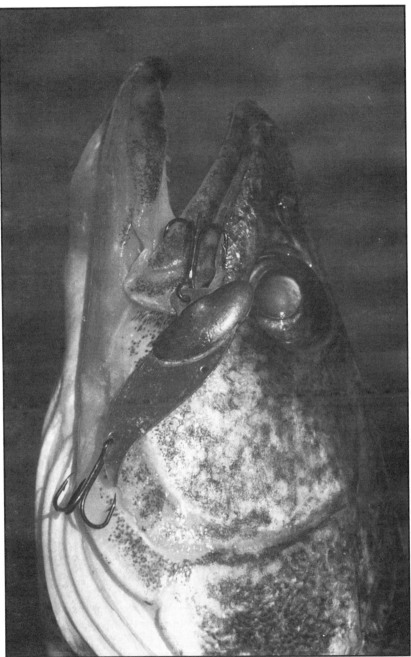

Tight-vibrating metal lures are just the ticket for small pockets in rivers.

This, of course, sets up lure and bait selection. If the fish are in the main channel and the current is tolerable, a jig worked on a near-vertical plane is unbeatable. But if the pocket is small and fairly deep, the current is apt to wash your jig by before it can sink into the hole.

Tight areas like this one, whether they're in the main channel or near the bank, call for a unique presentation. Fortunately, the perfect lure to get the job done exists: a Heddon Sonar (or a Gay Blade). These thin-bladed metal lures vibrate on a tight axis and can be vertically jigged in tight quarters; they'll dig *into* the current when yo-yoed below the boat, rather than get blown down-current. Naturally, the best way to pull this off is with good boat control by maintaining your position on top of the fish. Soon, a fish will smack that vibrator!

Swirling eddies are obvious fish-stackers, but they demand a closer look. If you don't fish them methodically, you could pass by a lot of fish. It's easy to do. Here's what could happen on a less than thorough going over.

Because most fish will be nose-to-the-current, your line must be dragged through the eddy from a number of different angles. It sounds elementary, but nine out of 10 guys make their casts from only one spot on the river by boat. Ultimately, their lure or bait will be detected too late for a fish to make a pass at it and return to the safety of its original position.

Here's where the bank fisherman has a distinct advantage. It's no big deal to flip a few casts at the cutting edge of the swirl, then move over and up to make another and another. Shortly, the entire eddy can be hit from a low profile efficiently and stealthily. Add this to the fact that many rivers lack decent boat launches, and many stretches are unnavigable, and you quickly realize that a pair of waders has its rightful place in any serious river fishing game plan.

What's the best presentation for eddies? Again, jigs are hands-down winners. But there's a common predicament linked to fishing jigs in rivers, especially along the swifter sections: The current swallows up your jig and puts a big belly in your line. The net result is little feel and even less control. To hurdle this obstacle, most anglers either give up or go to a heavier (3/8, 1/2 ounce) jig. This, of course, makes it tough for a walleye to suck it in.

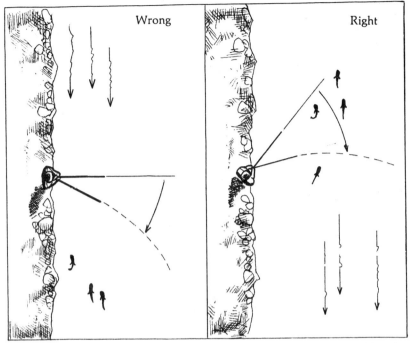

Bank fishermen (above) should always cast upstream and let the offering tumble toward the fish on a slack line. Likewise for anchored boats, below.

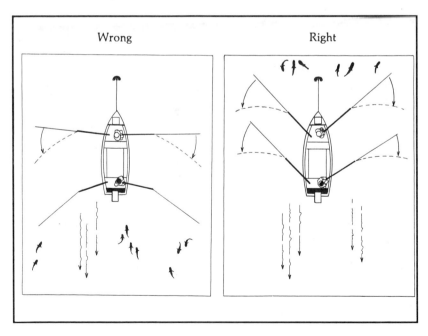

Mike takes a different tack. He has perfected a river jigging technique that not only lets him use comparatively light leadheads, but also adds longevity to his presentation. We call it "line-chasing" and it's very effective.

The key is to maintain your line in a vertical alignment at all times. When the current washes it to the left, you follow it with the boat and rod tip to the left. Ditto for any other direction. The best (and easiest) way to do this is with a bow-mounted electric trolling motor. Because you can also mount the transducer of your sonar on the shaft of the electric motor, you gain precise depth control, which can be critical in river situations.

Why is this so important? Another peculiarity of rivers is that very small places in the stream bed will hold a lot of fish; current breaks form behind bottom obstructions, and the fish pile in like fleas on a dog's tail. Being a few feet off the mark can really hurt because even river walleyes usually won't move more than a foot for dinner.

Learn to line-chase jigs in current, and other boats will be chasing you; saugers, like this one, should be easy prey.

As you chase your line, keep the power of your electric, or outboard, *at the same rate of flow* with the current. Common river rat tactics involve "slipping," where the boat drifts down-current, slightly *slower* than the river itself. This is okay for most river fishing, but line-chasing is better for three reasons. One, you will always be sitting on top of the fish, and hotspots are easier to detect. Two, less snags are the result because of the added control. And three, slipping adds some belly and straightens out the presentation in heavy current.

THE RACE IS ON: TAILRACES!

Tailraces below dams are becoming increasingly popular for the walleye "in" crowd and for good reason. Following new hydroelectric projects and the cleanup of industrialized rivers, resulting from irrigation projects and pollution abatement programs, respectively, new fisheries are springing up across the nation. Just as important, a good tailrace can sustain open-water action during freeze-up, giving hard-core anglers a welcomed alternative to icefishing.

Tailraces are fish magnets early and late in the season.

Most walleye fishermen new to the tailwater scene are easily intimidated by the current below the generators that swirls from a multitude of directions. Vertical jigging incorporating line chasing is practical in some of the large eddies, but be sure to tip your jigs. The walleyes below tailraces are accustomed to feeding on dead or injured minnows—smelt, spottail shiners, gizzard shad—that have been swept through the turbines. And the closer to the bottom (where current is reduced) you can maintain your drift, without getting hung up constantly, the better off you'll be.

Slab spoons (Hopkins Spoon, Kastmaster, etc.) have been around for decades, and they're appropriate whenever you've got a suspended forage base, or one where injured prey occasionally separate from the school and tumble toward the bottom. Recently, "swimming jigs" (Walleye Hawger, Rocker Minnow) have been hailed as "amazing baits" by a few zealous outdoor writers.

Slab spoons are an appropriate choice for tailwater saugers, too.

Don't be misled. There's nothing amazing about any lure or bait. To be effective, a lure simply must be fished where a fish can eat it. The main advantage of slab spoons and swimming jigs is that they duplicate the action of sporadic die-offs of suspended gizzard shad, alewives or smelt. Out of this environment, the lures' "sizzle" soon cools off!

One of the best ways to fish tailraces is with crankbaits. But it takes some foresight on precisely how to present them in the boiling current. Most anglers troll shallow-diving minnow-imitators upstream. Although this goes against the flow of how most fish are conditioned to receive their next meal, it can be effective. The water pushing against the bait creates an attractive action. And, if the trolling speed is only slightly faster than the current, many fish will be able to adjust to this unnatural angle of flight.

But there is a way to maximize your odds with crankbaits trolled upstream. Next time, instead of merely trolling in a straight line against the tailrace, try "lateral slipping." All you have to do is hold your position in the current and gently turn your outboard. The current will catch the shaft of the motor and your boat will angle to one side, without heading upstream or down. After you probe that area of the tailrace, turn your motor in the other direction, and cover the next swath. It's a great way to prospect for fish, as well as pinpoint their position in the tailrace. Then, it might be a good idea to work them over carefully with jigs. For tight fish, casting up-current (never down) or vertical line-chasing might be appropriate.

As you establish your trolling patterns, make note of exactly where each fish came from. Chances are excellent that there could be more walleyes lurking behind. And if you decide to pull up stakes, by all means don't run right over the fish. In the clear waters of most tailraces, walleyes can be spooky. Avoid suspected fish-holding pockets by motoring around them.

As effective as upstream trolling can be, there is a better method for trolling crankbaits, however. It incorporates the bottom bouncer, which really excels in tailrace fishing because it's about as snagless as you're going to find. In fact, the bottom bouncer was invented by a South Dakotan for precisely this application. Here's how to bottom-bounce a typical tailrace. Like many other techniques involved with tailrace fishing, there is a trick to it.

First, tie on a shallow-diving minnow-imitator with a "walleye wobble" to it. Use a leader length behind the sinker of about five or six feet. Next, lower the rig in the tailrace, *as you slowly drift downstream*, until you can feel bottom. Reel up a few inches and get ready to perform magic with the bait: Stroke your rod tip forward gently, following it back until the line straightens out again. Administer about a three or four-foot stroke, *and do it constantly.*

What happens if you don't? I'll relate an exasperating experience Mike and I suffered at the hands of a Pierre, South Dakota tailracaholic, Tim Carroll. You be the judge.

The three of us merrily trolled downstream in unison, below the Oahe Tailrace one December evening. Periodically, we'd get interrupted by Carroll's I've-got-another-one-get-the-net jab—bering. It was uncanny. After five fish to our one, I put the flashlight on his lure and sinker. Yup, he was using the exact same setup. As he lowered it into the drink, however, I put my rod down and eyed him with the intensity of a driver's training instructor. He was doing something different, all right, and in the dim light of the generator towers I could barely make it out.

"What's with all the rod sweeps?" I asked.

"I dunno," he said. "All I know is that one night I started doing it, and like magic I began to catch fish. I haven't quit since."

After following suit, both Mike and I started to get into the act. Afterward, we analyzed the situation and quickly realized that Carroll was onto something legitimate. We discovered that the current washed against our crankbaits when we trolled downstream. If we waited for a walleye to tell us he was there, we'd usually be too late; we missed at least a dozen fish that night before we finally landed one. But when we straightened the line out by pulling our rods forward, we took up the slack between the weight and the bait. This allowed us to detect strikes before the fish could spit the bait. It wasn't magic, just an effective presentation that let the fish eat and allowed us to know when they did.

This method of trolling minnow-imitators is so deadly in tailraces, you'll catch almost everything that swims on it, including salmon, trout, catfish, bass, eelpout and, of course, walleyes.

There's one more thing you ought to know about tailrace fishing. A common fallacy involving walleyes and waterflow has been floating around lately: That fish "disperse" in low-water conditions, and "concentrate" upstream once the spillways

Saugeye, a natural sauger/walleye cross, are quite at home in rivers and tailraces.

are opened and the current increases. A radio-tagging study done by South Dakota biologist, Jim Riis, proved otherwise.

Riis implanted four walleyes with ultrasonic transmitters and released them at Oahe Tailrace. Much to his surprise, the fish didn't move more than a quarter-mile all summer, in spite of fluctuating water levels below the dam. Moreover, his crews were unable to locate one of the tagged fish—it took up residence among some dead trees.

Riis finally found it in three feet of water.

CHAPTER 18
IN THE DARK ABOUT WALLEYES?

No walleye book would be complete without covering night fishing. In the chapter, *The Truth About WallEYES*, we nailed down the real reason why night fishing can be effective: It's a *condition* that allows anglers to fish walleyes before they spook them. It has little to do with being a "magic moment" or a "peak feeding time" that "requires certain lures or baits." Ironically, a lot of information on the subject deals with just that—presentations geared specifically for this time slot. Fact is, any daytime tactic will work on nighttime fish, so what's all the fuss? Do the fish suddenly switch their diet or go through a mood swing?

You know better. So instead of talking about what lures work best in the dark, we'll steer you in another direction: tackling unforeseen obstacles that are sure to crop up when the sun goes down. A good after-dark strategy should include three components: which waters, when to hit them, and preparation for the battle.

It's no secret that some fisheries are better than others under the wrap of darkness. Tailraces offer a classic night bite, but they aren't the only one. Like the Jekyll-Hyde twilight bite, some waters instantly turn on, while others are a total bust then. You just have to know which is which.

Generally, most clear waters are candidates for the graveyard shift. Weak daytime winds seem to accentuate the phenomenon. Conversely, you should avoid turbid waters like someone with halitosis; stained waters typically peak during midday, unless a cold front hits. Besides tailraces, check out Canadian shield lakes and heavily developed recreation lakes. Daytime activity—speedboating, water-skiing, snorkeling—serve to put fish into a nocturnal cadence.

Another daytime sleeper is the bass/panfish lake that has received incidental stockings of walleye fingerlings. These shallow, dishpan lakes are typically choked with weeds, making daylight fishing difficult, if not downright impossible. To boot, the walleyes may have adjusted to nocturnal feeding patterns to avoid bass predation. Fortunately, once the sun sets, the fish not only leave the cover of the salad bar, but they put the feed bag on.

Timing can impact your night fishing significantly. Moon phases, solunar tables and weather all interact and affect feeding schedules. It is a commonly accepted belief that new moon and full moon periods are best for big fish. Our experiences do not match up with this theory. (We've caught some mighty nice fish below a quarter or half-moon!) Bob Propst, who has put in more time on the water after dark than anyone else, goes fishing when the weather is favorable and when he can squeeze it in. He doesn't let a chart or moon phase dictate his schedule. We're like-minded on the subject. There are a few principles involving evening patterns, however, that are worth considering.

One is that stable weather will allow you to get a handle on when fish in a particular water body are likely to turn on throughout the night. The fish get into a certain cycle, and our observations indicate that if weather systems don't screw things up, the fish invariably will turn on within an hour of their feeding time the previous night. Most of the time this will be a little later on each successive evening. So if the fish bit on Insomnia Lake Chain at midnight on Saturday evening, they'll probably turn on Sunday night a little later—about 12:30 or 1:00 a.m.

What about that moon? Is a full moon a good time to go walleye fishing? Bob says "Usually not." We agree. The added light may help you tie up a dandy Surgeon's Sling knot, but it will make the fish unapproachable if there aren't any waves. Ah, waves. Now that changes everything, day and night. Without exception, you'll catch zillions more fish at night if there's a good chop. And we're talking about one that borders on being uncomfortable to fish in. About three feet is ideal.

Shoreline structure, particularly drop-offs off associated with points, can be good at night. Mark Martin makes a good living guiding guests with this pattern, and he obviously does quite well with it on Michigan's Muskegon Lake, where he took third in a 1988 MWC tournament held there. Martin, like Propst, would rather stay home and rest up if the conditions aren't right.

"Nothing is worse than flat calm seas beneath the man in the moon," Martin says. "Even with a stiff wind and healthy waves, I like to use my electric motor exclusively at night when trolling."

Martin prospects for fish while he fishes, in order to establish a pattern for the evening. Then he hits those honey holes hard. If you've got shallow-water fish, there's a shortcut to the business of fish-finding at night. Frankly, it's so easy, we're amazed so few anglers employ the technique. All you need is a Q-Beam spotlight. Recall that Mike uses the tactic for finding shallow-water fish for the following day (see Chapter 9). It works equally well for locating fish in the evening! The only difference is that you can't motor up and start working over the fish you've just zapped with the spotlight. You've got to rest them for at least an hour. Chances are good they'll still be there, and now that you've got them pinpointed, you should be able to hook a few. Incidentally, individual night spots will be good time and time again—not just the first evening.

Preparation is another key to successful night fishing. Fishing at night won't be as easy as daytime fishing but, if you make the necessary adjustments, you can get the job done without busting too many graphite rods, or nicking the prop up, or losing a case of crankbaits, or...

For starters, never hit unfamiliar territory after dark. Arrive in plenty of time to scope it out and get a feel for the layout of the area to be fished. For tailraces, pay particular attention to the shallow spots, and how the water flows when different gates are opened. A sudden surge of water can change current direction and catch you off guard. This is eerie enough during the day. At night, your heebie-jeebies might develop into a severe case of the screaming meemies.

On paper, the notion of catching walleyes at night looks to be an easy undertaking, once the fish are located. It's not. A reef you've fished a hundred times becomes a mystery under the cloak of darkness when you can't see beyond your rod tip; familiar waters turn into foreign seas after nightfall.

A detailed map—hand drawn by daylight—of each area you intend to fish is indispensable. Make note of anything unique about each target that could help keep you on location. A cabin, a large rock, or a crooked tree could be just the benchmark you need. I remember one stretch of shoreline that was indistinguishable from the surrounding area, except for a small bird's nest in a bush. It turned out to be a handy reference point—all our fish came within 10 feet, either side of it.

In your map-making project, don't forget navigation routes. Once I got so caught up in charting an island, I forgot about marking the route down. I ended up lost in a back bay for two hours before I finally got my bearings. It's surprising how friendly bays can become foreboding, giant mouse traps at night. A simple trick on large bodies of water (especially island-studded Canadian shield lakes) is to count each bay or island you pass enroute. It will keep you on course.

In waters described above, reefs offer some of the best, if not *the* best nighttime fishing. Why? Two reasons. First, both resident and nomadic fish (remember the Chautauqua Lake telemetry study) should be present. Also, precise depth control—a must during the day—isn't quite so crucial; evening fish tend to "roam" off the bottom much more than those during the day.

Joe Bucher with a dandy nighttime Wisconsin walleye. Photo by Joe Bucher.

Still, it helps to know where the top and the drop-offs of the reef are. There's no better way than with marker buoys. Discarded bleach containers (spray-painted different colors for differing depths) really help.

Lighting can be a touchy subject. The Coast Guard has their requirements and so do individual fishermen. Our advice is the same as with jig weight and line diameter: less is best. You'll need a "night light" jury-rigged for your boat to handle sticky situations, such as examining frayed line or landing a trophy fish. A simple painter's lamp (the kind with rubber-lined clamps) with a 12-volt bulb drawing juice from your marine battery should suffice. On calm nights you might have to cover it with a handkerchief.

An overlooked nighttime convenience is a miner's head lamp. It can be flipped on quickly and shines exactly where you're looking.

Your night life will greatly improve if you keep a flashlight right where everyone knows it will be. Be sure not to move it without saying so. While you're at it, try taping a small penlight to the landing net's handle, and put some reflective tape (or phosphorescent tape) on the tip of the net. It's difficult enough keeping track of someone else's fish in the dark, without having to wonder where the landing net is in relation to the fish. A final touch would be to put a little tape on your rod tip. Last but not least, don't forget the Q-Beam spotlight for emergencies.

And don't forget to dress warm. Layers of extra clothing are just as important as your rod and reel. Who can fish very well when they're miserably cold? When the sun sets, the thermometer can really take a drop, especially over a lake's surface. An insulated RefrigiWear one-piece, coupled with rain gear would be ideal for early and late-season excursions.

The best nighttime tactic and presentation? A simple one. By now it should be clear that the mathematical edge goes to the presentation that puts in the most time, fishing-wise. Artificials have a decided advantage over live bait. It's hard to beat floating minnow-imitators, since you can't cast them off, and they run at the same depths every time you put them out. Moreover, they're relatively maintenance-free, allowing you to concentrate on running the boat and keeping on track.

This translates into another tip: Don't clutter up the boat with half a dozen rods, four tackle boxes, and three buckets of live bait. Decide what you're going to do ahead of time and stick to it. Keep it simple. Things you step around during the day get stepped on at night. Remember, your night fishing will only be as effective as it is hassle-free.

Also, use closed-face reels for after-dark fishing. Although you might have graduated to an open-face reel, it's time to "regress" and go with a spin-cast model. It could save you many moments of anguish.

Lastly, a word of encouragement to the weak and unbelieving. If you've never seen a stringer of marble eyes after dark, drop by a popular landing where experienced anglers are likely to be coming in with their evening catches. Seeing success with your own eyes will cure your skepticism, once and for all. What did it for me was an unforgettable encounter I had with an old-timer at the public dock, many years ago.

"Boy, they must've been hitting tonight," I said, admiring his hefty stringer.

"Nope," he said around his cigar.

"But those are some pretty nice fish," I said.

Slightly annoyed, he peered at me and replied, "You should have seen last night's stringer, sonny."

CHAPTER 19
A TOUGH QUESTION

T he main thrust of our approach to the game of walleye fishing is pretty straightforward—find the hottest fish as soon as possible, and work them over with the most efficient presentation. That usually means hop-scotching from spot to spot. Over the long run, it simply outfishes every other approach to the game.

But there are exceptions.

A prime example of this is the 1988 MWC Championship, held in mid-September on the Mississippi River near Dubuque, Iowa. Mike and Bob finished second, a fish out of first behind Gary Parsons and his partner. Jerry Anderson and his teammate finished a close third. The rest of the pack fell considerably behind these three, and it would be profitable to examine the strategies each used, and then analyze the situation.

Each team pre-fished the tournament boundaries and came up with what they felt were their best spots to concentrate on during the contest. Gary Parsons made "milk runs" all three days to his six key spots, while Mike and Bob did the same on seven spots. Jerry Anderson tried the milk run approach on the first day but was dissatisfied with the results, and he decided to "camp" on the piece of structure he felt might produce the biggest fish. Here are the interesting results:

• Parsons "hit it right," catching fish from several key areas, mostly flooded wingdams; when the fish decided to bite he was there. His milk run approach was a gamble, and it paid off. Luck—mostly in terms of timing—aided his hard-fought victory.

• Mike and Bob also went the milk run route. Unfortunately, many of their best areas "didn't go" during the tournament. It seemed that just as they left, another boat would pull in (one time it was Parsons) and yank in a fish or two. Yet, Lady Luck didn't abandon the guys entirely. After all, they did take second.

For example, on the last day of the three-day event, Mike and Bob exhausted their resources. Late in the afternoon they were fishless, after hitting their six "top prospects." On a whim, they tried a seventh spot—a hump in the arm of the river. They had pre-fished it but hadn't tried it during the tournament because there were other boats on it, and no fish showed up on the sonar. At first, they trolled bottom bouncers and crawler harnesses. After several short-hits, they decided to lighten up and toss eighth-ounce jigs tipped with a piece of a crawler

What happened? It's interesting what timing can do for you. The guys took 15 fish in the next 30 minutes, of which eight were big enough to weigh in.

• Anderson's camping tactics over a single piece of structure produced consistent, but not spectacular results this time around (you might recall that he won the 1986 MWC Championship with a similar tactic). Among other things, Anderson noted that the fish bit four times throughout the day, and each "bite" lasted precisely 10 minutes. This occurred on both the second and third day he tried camping.

Conclusions? One fishery a hard-and-fast rule does not make. You have to realize that this experience stems from a system whose forage population was at an all-time high; the fish had no trouble filling their gullets, and short feeding bursts are the rule, not the exception.

Exactly why the fish turn on when they do is a mystery, but Mike's explanation is as good as any: "It's like people sitting in a room when someone starts yawning. Pretty soon, another person yawns too. Before long, everybody within 'yawning distance' will have gotten into the act. It's contagious."

By the same token, it's "catchy" when one fish decides to bite. Others seem to follow suit for short, intense bursts. It's mindful of the slip bobber frenzy Parsons shared earlier. Keep this unusual pattern in mind when fishing a system with a lot of feed in it. Timing can be important, and camping, a la Jerry Anderson style, will always yield consistent, if not overwhelming results. But you have to be patient; it could be a long wait. More important, better make sure that your "tent pad" is currently holding fish.

CHAPTER 20
COMING TO TERMS:
A GLOSSARY OF DEFINITIONS

Although fishermen often sport dirty fingernails, and are regularly accused of s-t-r-e-t-c-h-i-n-g the truth, perhaps their worst fault is using terms that are either bigger than they are, or are downright confusing. Walleye lingo has taken some strange detours on the road to clear communication.

Our favorite example of this is "inside turn." It's usually where a point meets the shoreline. But since most points have two inside turns (one on each side) wouldn't it be wiser to call such key spots "elbows"? We like "cups," because it's a more accurate description of a unique place that "holds" fish.

Hence, a chronic need for clear definitions. The following glossary may be a bit creative, but it's meant to be a common-sense, down to earth attempt at saying exactly what we mean, and meaning exactly what we say. It's short but complete.

Alley: Specific movement lanes of fish on reefs or in weeds.

Ambush feeding: How walleyes eat; typically by hiding with structure as an aid.

Backtrolling: A method of boat control that pulls, not pushes, the boat from the stern.

Bottom bouncer: Particularly snagless sinker with the lead weight fashioned to a 10-inch feeler wire.

Bulking up: Adding mass to a jig with oversized dressings.

Calendar of live bait: The erroneous assumption that fish choose certain baits at certain times of the year.

Cannonball: A heavy lead weight used in conjunction with downrigger fishing.

Coiled leader: See Memory leader.

Cold fish: A walleye with a very negative mood and a very small strike zone.

Contour cutting: Running across, not alongside, drop-offs at relatively high speeds with sonar.

Contour tracking: Boat control that follows a specific depth wherever it goes.

Crankbait: Artificial lure designed to dive when trolled or retrieved.

Cup: Unfortunately called "inside turns." Means a specific place where underwater contours suddenly bend together to form walls on three sides.

Dipping: Dropping a bait with a long pole into heavy cover such as brush or weedbeds.

Dunking: Presenting a jig so that it lies motionless on the bottom for extended periods.

Eaters: Walleyes in the 1-1/2 to 2-pound range; the only fish modern anglers should keep.

Fishing (defined): Occurs only when a fish can eat someone's lure or bait.

Fishing pressure: The result of fishing and boating activity; usually negative, never positive.

Frenzy: Heightened fish activity incited and snowballed by feeding fish.

Going fishing: Having the appearance, but never the results, of fishing.

Hook set: The act of applying pressure to displace a fish.

Hot fish: Suicidal fish with a large strike zone.

Hydraulics: Unique properties of a bait that apparently make it more appealing to gamefish than its look-alike clones.

Jig: A hook with a lead weight molded to its eye.

Jigging: Up and down action applied to a lure or bait.

Lateral line: Sensory organ of fish that allows them to "feel" movement and distinguish objects.

Lateral slipping: Boat control in rivers best suited for fishing crankbaits upstream.

L-serine: Amino acid present in humans; detected in minute traces by some fish.

Lukewarm fish: Catchable fish with an expandable strike zone.

Lindy rigging: System of fishing live bait with a slip sinker.

Line chasing: Using boat control to maintain a vertical presentation in current.

Long rod: Fishing pole longer than six feet; typically nine or 10 feet.

Longevity of presentation: Length of time a lure or bait is placed within a fish's strike zone.

Memory leader: Sections of old fishing line from a reel that unspools in spring-like coils.

Presentation: How a tactic is employed; specifically how a lure or bait is offered to a fish.

Prospecting: Going fishing while looking for fish.

Radio-tracking (radio telemetry): The use of ultrasonic equipment for monitoring fish movements.

Reef: Shallow water surrounded on all sides by deeper water; underwater island.

Release: Device used to temporarily hold line until a fish strikes; attached to tow cords, trolling boards, downrigger cables or cannonballs.

Secondary rods (tuna rig): Additional rod(s) allowed by some state regulations having the following attributes: generally unattended, placed in a rod holder, rigged as snag-free as possible.

Shining: Fish-locating technique involving spotlighting fish during calm seas at night.

Slip bobber: A hollow, free-sliding float used in conjunction with an adjustable stop.

Slipping: Boat control in rivers that flows with the current at a slightly slower rate.

Spawn, pre-spawn, post-spawn: Specific periods during the spring spawning season.

Speed trolling: Boat control with artificials at an accelerated rate of travel.

Staging areas: Place near spawning sites that fish congregate prior to spawning.

Strike zone: The vertical and horizontal distance a fish will travel to take a lure or bait.

Structure: Any change in depth or in bottom composition that attracts fish on a regular basis.

Tactic: Method of presenting a bait or lure (trolling, jigging, casting etc.).

Twilight bite: The short, intense feeding period correlating to dusk and dawn.

INDEX